SAINT EPHREM

AN EXPOSITION OF THE GOSPEL

CORPUS

SCRIPTORUM CHRISTIANORUM ORIENTALIUM

EDITUM CONSILIO

UNIVERSITATIS CATHOLICAE AMERICAE

ET UNIVERSITATIS CATHOLICAE LOVANIENSIS

Vol. 292

SCRIPTORES ARMENIACI

TOMUS 6

SAINT EPHREM

AN EXPOSITION OF THE GOSPEL

TRANSLATED

BY

GEORGE A. EGAN

LOUVAIN

SECRÉTARIAT DU CorpusSCO

49, CH. DE WAVRE

1968

INTRODUCTION

The treatise translated here was originally written in Syriac by St. Ephrem (d. 373 A.D.), and was later translated by ancient Armenian translators. At present, it is extant only in two Armenian MSS (No. 452, No. 312), located in the manuscript library of the Armenian monastery of San Lazzaro, in Venice. For details concerning these MSS and other bibliographical material concerning this treatise, see the Introduction to Volume I.

Some study has been done previously of this treatise by some scholars, mainly Schäfers, but these studies were based on only one manuscript. The result of these studies was that the treatise was set aside as not a genuine Ephrem writing. But further study by the author, and the addition of a second manuscript, has shown that this treatise is evidently an authentic Ephrem document. For a discussion of its authenticity see the Introduction to Volume I.

This treatise is very similar in style and content, to the Diatessaron Commentary written by St. Ephrem. In fact, it is attached to the ending of that Commentary, in the two MSS which contain the Armenian version of the Commentary. Until recently, that Commentary was extant only in Armenian version, and only in the two MSS mentioned. It is with regret that the recently found MS of the Syriac original of the Commentary (Cf. Chester Beatty Monographs, No. 8 : *Saint Ephrem*, Commentaire de l'Évangile Concordant; edited by L. Leloir, Dublin, 1963), did not continue, so that we might have had the original Syriac to this treatise also. But perhaps this will also turn up some day soon.

'An Exposition of the Gospel' abounds with many quotations from the Old Testament and the New Testament, and which contain many distinctive, early readings of the Biblical text. Volume III, in the Subsidia, is devoted to an analysis of the Biblical quotations. This treatise, therefore, is important not only to the study of early Christian thought, but more so to the study of the history of the Biblical text.

The translation of the Armenian text into English, given in this volume, is not purely literal, as this would not give the proper meaning many times. In order for the translation to be of textual value, all paraphrasing is avoided as much as possible. Idiomatic expressions are properly rather than literally translated, whenever some authority, i.e. a dictionary, grammar or Biblical usage, has been found for it. Sometimes conjunctions are altered or omitted in order to make sentences complete and coherent. The 'number' of verbs (or nouns) occasionally is modified in order to be put into proper English. Relative pronouns are always translated. The excessive use of *ասէ* (he says), to indicate a quotation, is always translated, but to simplify the reading, if it occurs within a quotation it is put before the quotation. Although it tends to make the translation seem somewhat 'rough' at times, key words and expressions are translated as closely as possible to the meaning of the Armenian in its context. By these means it is hoped to preserve the style of the original.

Words supplied for clarification, i.e. not in the Armenian text, are put in parentheses. It should also be said that for obvious reasons the punctuation in the translation does not necessarily follow the punctuation in the Armenian text, though this is minimized as much as possible.

The method of presenting variants is the same as used with the Armenian text; see Volume I and its Introduction. The primary text is from Codex A, and the variants to it from Codex B are in the first apparatus at the bottom of the page; the first apparatus also includes the explanatory notes, which are indicated by lower case letters of the alphabet; the second apparatus contains the Biblical references. The bracket 'Γ' used in connection with the variants does not apply to the 'lettered' explanatory notes, even though such an indication may occur within a variant of more than one word.

It should also be pointed out that the apparatus containing the variants is not simply a literal translation of the variants under the Armenian text. The Armenian variants have been 'inserted' into the Armenian text and the text is then retranslated and the differences from the original translation (i.e. the translation of Codex A) are then listed as variants from Codex B. For example, if an Armenian variant was simply a different word meaning the same thing as the word in the text (Codex A), then no variant would appear at that point in the translation.

The primary text is generally the 'preferred' text; see Introduction to Volume I for the basis for this decision, and also for the method of indicating preferred readings among the variants. It should be emphasized here, as in the variants to the Armenian text, a 'preferred reading', though it is in the apparatus, it should be considered as though it were in the primary text. The text cannot be properly read, many times, without the 'preferred reading'.

The Biblical quotations which are given in the second apparatus, are indicated according to the number of the line of the text in which the quotation starts and by means of special symbols. When a reference contains a verse, or verses, which are not fully quoted, the reference is usually followed by 'a' or 'b', indicating which half of the verse is available. Occasionally a long verse is divided into three parts, whereupon a third letter 'c' is brought into use, thus indicating which 'third', or 'thirds', of the verse are available.

The location of marginal readings, which appear only in Codex A, are indicated by lower case letters. These are given at the appropriate place in the apparatus for the variants. A marginal reading is preceded by the abbreviation 'MR'.

For consistency, the Biblical references are always numbered according to the text of the original language of the appropriate section of the Bible. The quotations from the Old Testament are given according to the versification of the Hebrew (*Biblia Hebraica.* Rud. Kittel, editor. Stuttgart, 1949), and those from the New Testament are given according to the Greek (*Novum Testamentum Graeca.* D.E. Nestle, editor. Stuttgart, 1948).

In the appendices there are two lists of Biblical quotations, one in the order in which they occur in the treatise (Appendix A) and a second list in the order of the books of the Bible (Appendix B). The first list includes all of the quotations, allusions, etc., but the second list contains only the quotations which are covered in the critical analysis, i.e. in the *Subsidia* (Vol. III). There are four quotations, all from the New Testament, which occur only in Codex B. These are given in both lists and are indicated as such.

*

* *

AN EXPOSITION OF THE GOSPEL

1. All books whichever [1] are written from the minds of men and speak not from the Law and the Prophets, (such) books are the production and creation of opposing minds. And [2] if anyone approaches to examine their minds, he finds them heretical and wavering because they are not based on the true foundation of the Holy Scriptures. Marcion writes in his book which they indeed named Προευαγγελιον, that is, translated into our language it is called 'Before the Gospels', and I have wondered how could there be a book of the Marcionites which they indeed named 'Before the Gospels', when his disciples hopefully think [3] that the beginning of the divinity in which they believe appeared at those times, in the years of Pontius Pilate, at the time in which the Gospels were written [4]. If it is true for you, O Marcion, that truly the beginning of the divinity concerning which you speak was from the Gospels, really how or in what manner can your book be before the Gospels? And if you are truly affirmed and [5] your book could be before the Gospels, do not say that the life-giving divinity emanated recently and strangely [6], but he was in fact already here. And it is written [7] in the beginning of the book in this manner, it says, 'O the exceeding greatness, ⌐the folly, the power [8], and the wonders, for there is nothing to say about it, nor to think concerning it, and there is nothing to render like unto it'.

2. Now let us leave aside all his books and against this thing let us say that this [1] what you say, Marcion, certainly [2] (is) true, it is not manifested by the tongue, nor is it explained through thoughts, and nothing resembles it. Now silence! and speak not concerning that which you yourself have insisted upon and say, that it is not manifested, nor are there thoughts concerning it, nor does it resemble anything. How much Marcion lied I will show, for ⌐he speaks not from the true foundation. The Lord says [3] in his Gospels, that [4]

---

1. [1] which. — [2] om. — [3] read. — [4] add : 'and' B. — [5] that. — [6] strange voice. — [7] + moreover. — [8] read : 'the wisdom of the power' B.

2. [1] that. — [2] now also (it). — [3] spoke (not) from the truth and our Lord taught. — [4] + his.

faith in various matters is like everything whatever is of this world.
He says in this manner that it is like a building, wine, a garment, fire,
seeds, a kingdom, silver, ⌜a talent [5], ⌜a plant [6], a grain of mustard-seed,
and [7] leaven.　Now how is anyone able to listen to the Gospel which
says, faith with its aspects is like all these things and in the meantime 5
listen to Marcion who says, it is not like anything?　And how it is
like all those things, I show just now.

　　3.　It is like buildings; because like ⌜a building [1], they are brought
together by many works [2]; ⌜it is composed of parts [a],[3] and becomes
a house.　In like manner also, we of all races, and of all languages, 10
and of all kingdoms, and of all minds, are brought together, and [4] we
become one mind [5], a completed people, a holy tent, a camp of God.
Moreover it is like buildings [6]; because when man ⌜constructs a building [7], he does not despise concerning all the necessities; whatever
⌜may be [8] necessary for material for the buildings [9], he gathers, and 15
brings stone, wood ⌜and reeds [10], earth, and iron and [11] copper, and
of all the things of necessity for material for the building.　But if
he despises each [12] of those, then [13] his building will not be crowned
with accomplishment.　In like manner also, it is not right for us to
despise, because we build faith through fasting [14], through holiness [15], 20
through giving gifts [b], and through visiting the sick, through loving [16]
the brethern, and [17] through worship of God, and by attending church,
and by praying continually, and by considering the mysteries in the
Scriptures.　And [18] if we despise any one of these, moreover neither
will our faith be built.　But as those by whom the building is made 25
do not sleep, as also [19] David himself says : 'I will not give sleep to †
my eyes nor slumber to my eye lids, until I shall make a temple for
the Lord and a place of abode for the God of Jacob'; in like manner
also, we are obliged to run by day, and ⌜to watch and to be vigilant [20]
by night with prayers and supplications, so that we also shall be built 30

---

[5] om. — [6] plants. — [7] om.
　　3.　[1] buildings. — [2] materials. — [a] or : members. — [3] and it is assembled of many parts.
— [4] om. — [5] house. — [6] a building. — [7] becomes a building. — [8] (things) are. — [9] building. — [10] bricks. — [11] om. — [12] read : 'one' B. — [13] om. — [14] holiness. — [15] fasting. —
[b] i.e. tithes and offerings. — [16] visiting. — [17] om. — [18] but. — [19] om. — [20] by night also
to watch and to be vigilant by day and.

　　3.　† Ps 132:4,5.

on the foundation of the Apostles and the Prophets, as also [21] the
Apostle says, for if they who build earthly houses do give themselves
to labor [22] in order that they might make their shelters [23] for a few
years, but we make an eternal camp for our souls and a house of
5 praise to heaven, it is more necessary for us to work and labor.

4. And as they who make buildings are never ashamed when
anyone may watch them — for they may pull up reeds and cut wood
and roll stones and carry [1] rocks, and it is not possible to hide their
works — in like manner also, it is not right for ⌐any of [2] us to be
10 ashamed of this good, handsome fruit which we make, and it is not
possible for us to hide, while we [3] attend church, and visit the sick
and give gifts [a], and pray and fast; and if anyone is ashamed of these,
he can not be a part of the divine building. But they ⌐who construct
buildings [4], although the building itself is not hid, nevertheless not
15 in order that their [5] brethren might see them [6] and praise them [7],
⌐do they [8] labor (and) offer whatever ⌐may be [9] necessary for material
for the building, but they work and labor for themselves. Moreover
the outsiders see that [10] they work not in order that they ⌐might be
praised [11] by men. In like manner also, it is not right for us to hide,
20 and we ought not to take [12] anew so that men might see and praise us,
and we should not run for the praise of others. But as some men,
⌐we do mercies for ourselves [13], and others who might meet us will
see that we labor not for them.

5. ⌐And as [1] those by whom ⌐buildings are [2] made, are urged
25 to build and complete everything in the summer-time, that they
may be under shelter and may rest in the winter-days [3], ⌐because
the summer-days are for buildings [4]. But he who in the summer-
days does not make his [5] buildings, disgrace and outrage [a] will reach
him in the winter-days. And as the time for buildings is set (as)
30 the summer-days, in like manner ⌐is set [6] the time of our habitation
which is here in the world, in order to go and hasten [7] and make for
us a habitation in heaven. And he who in this time does not prepare

---

[21] om. — [22] + to toils and to vigilance. — [23] dwellings.

4. [1] beat. — [2] om. — [3] om. — [a] e.g. tithes. — [4] he who constructs a building. —
[5] his. — [6] him. — [7] him. — [8] did he. — [9] is. — [10] om. — [11] praise them. — [12] read :
'make' B. — [13] they would think to do mercies for themselves.

5. [1] as also. — [2] a building is. — [3] winter-times. — [4] om. — [5] (his). — [a] or : insults. —
[6] has been. — [7] with haste.

and make his place of abode with the righteous, after his death he
cannot make or prepare his [8], because [9] it is not possible ⌜for buildings
to be made [10] in the winter-days.   And with this parable with which
our Lord likened his faith to the buildings of men, he fulfilled [11] the
word of prophecy [12].   Isaiah says, 'But Zion said, the [13] Lord aban- †
doned me and [14] God forgot me.   Is it not possible (that) a woman might
forget her babe [15], or [16] (that) she might not be moved to compassion
on the child of her womb; and perhaps a woman might forget this,
nevertheless I shall not forget [17], says the Lord.   Behold on my
hands I pictured [18] your walls and before my eyes you are all the 10
time'.

    6. Moreover David says, 'The stone which the builders despised †
became the chief [a] corner (stone) of the buildings [1]; by the Lord it
became this'.   And Paul takes this from the Prophet and the Gospels;
he says [2], 'Christ himself (is) [3] the chief corner (stone) of the building, ⊙
through which all the building is joined and fitted'.   ⌜And he makes
clear that we who have believed are the building [4], and Christ [5] the
chief corner (stone) of the building.   And ⌜David was not [6] ⌜the
corner [7], for ⌜one wall of the buildings was made in him, only circumcision [8].   ⌜Now since Christ preached circumcision and uncircum- 20
cision [9], two walls were made from him and he became [10] the head [b].
And how or in what manner he became a despised stone, in the Gospels
it says, 'It is necessary for the Son of Man to pass through much ◐
sufferings [11], to be scorned and to be despised by the elders and by the
scribes' [c].   And [12] because the name of the stone is not far from it, 25
the Apostle himself says [13] concerning the spiritual stone which gave
to drink to the sons of Israel : ⌜'But that [14] stone is Christ himself'. ☥
He, even Simon whom Christ left, in his place [d], he called him [15] in

---

[8] om. — [9] as. — [10] to make buildings. — [11] fulfills. — [12] + which. — [13] my. — [14] +
my. — [15] babes. — [16] and. — [17] add : 'you' B. — [18] shall picture.
    6.   [a] or : head. — [1] the building. — [2] add : 'Jesus' B. — [3] is. — [4] om. — [5] + is. —
[6] not David. — [7] om. — [8] he only in circumcision became the wall of the building. —
[9] but Christ, the corner-stone, because circumcision and uncircumcision were preached
by him. — [10] is. — [b] or : chief. — [11] + and. — [c] word in Codex here literally means
'judges', but the word can also mean 'lawyer', which is also one meaning of the Syriac
word for 'scribes'. — [12] om. — [13] was saying. — [14] the. — [d] lit. lit. instead of him. —
[15] + a rock.

    5.   † Isa 49:14-16.
    6.   † Ps 118:22,23a. — ⊙ Eph 2:20b,21. — ◐ Lk 9:22. — ☥ I Cor 10:4c.

order that he might lead his church.   And on these parables of the
Prophets, the Church was established [16] in the likeness of buildings [17].

7.   ⌜Therefore our Lord likened his faith to buildings [1], in that
† he says, 'Everyone who comes to me and [2] hears my words and does
5 them [3], is [a] like a wise man who built his house : he digged and deepened, and laid the foundation upon rugged rock'.   ⌜And because
he says, he digged and deepened [4], in this way he makes clear to us
that [5] the renewal and stability which the instruction of the teaching
embraces, not only did it indeed come to us, but it was ⌜in fact [6]
10 within us at one time.   And as I [7] shall continue to dig, how [8] can
we stand on the truth, if it had not reached us from the Father from
the beginning from all eternity ?   And when we shall look to the rock
yonder to the stone which we have allegorized, and we see that it is
fixed before his creation, and when it indeed falls down, its base is
15 ground from the falling and the grinding, and the artisan [b] takes a
strong tool of iron and he digs (and) takes from it the superfluous
earth and ground soil [c], and he [9], puts his foundation on rugged,
solid rock, which is able to endure the force of buildings [10].   In like
manner also, in our childhood we were pure and innocent in the
20 teaching of divinity, and [11] as ⌜the stability of our truth [d] decays [12]
in the licentiousness of fornication and sensuality of folly, then we
are not able to endure the force of [13] the foundation of the building.

8.   But when we take in our hand the Gospel of redemption [a] in
the likeness of iron [b], and we gather (and) remove from us all these [1]
25 works of evil, and then we put the foundation of faith on our hearts,
on rugged rock, when our minds shall be purified of all evil, and [2]
when the foundations of the building are established, thenceforth [3]
we also [4] become laborers [c] and artisans [d].   And ⌜for example [5],
everything whatever may be lacking to the artisan, there is nowhere [6]

---

[16] made. — [17] the building.
    7.   [1] om. — [2] om. — [3] these. — [a] lit. was (copyist error). — [4] om. — [5] om. — [6] om. —
[7] read : 'we' B. — [8] there. — [b] i.e. skilled-worker; lit. architect. — [c] lit. dirt. — [9] add:
'takes (and)' B. — [10] building. — [11] om. — [d] or : sincerity. — [12] we fell from the stability
of our truth. — [13] and.
    8.   [a] MR : truth. — [b] probably an iron tool, e.g. shovel. — [1] om. — [2] om. — [3] om. —
[4] om. — [c] i.e. field-workers. — [d] i.e. skilled workers; lit. architects. — [5] om. — [6] + else.

    7.   † Lk 6:47,48a.

for him to go, except to the doors of the master of the work. In like
manner also let us know ⌜that he is wealthy, this one [7] who is the
master of our work, from whom we received the pledge to make
these buildings for him. For whatever material for the work of life
may be lacking for us, from him let us ask : holiness, mercy, love, 5
cheerfulness, ⌜brotherly love [8], and he personally gives to us abundantly from his good treasures [9] with his hand, when we press his
doors and ask from him [10]. ⌜And in all this the teaching of our Lord
is likened to buildings [11].

9.   And [1] moreover our [2] Lord likened his faith to wine, in that 10
he says, 'No one puts new [3] wine into old [a] leather bottles, otherwise †
the new wine bursts the old leather bottles, the wine is poured out
and the leather bottles are destroyed : but they put new wine into
new leather bottles'. Now what perhaps may they think, they who
may imitate ? Is it possible (that) the innovation ⌜may be [4] foreign 15
to antiquity ? Perhaps they [5] may think that the old leather bottles
are old originally and have [6] never been new. It is clear to every
man, that when God [7] created them, or when [8] their author [b] made

---

[7] him. — [8] om. — [9] works. — [10] + But when he completes the work of the building,
always alert and courageous, with precaution, he takes care lest in the rainy season
having become wet from the roofs being caved in, the waters freely drip down; and
from that time they who shall be in the house will go outside; because they do not suffer
patiently the unpleasant sight of the dripping waters which by a fellow-laborer is seen
on the ceiling. In like manner also, when we hear the instruction of the teaching of
our Lord and we are made his divine habitation, it is necessary for us from that time
to cut and cleanse (ourselves) by fasts and prayers and confession; lest the sensuality
of impurity as accumulated clouds will strongly rain on us, and scatters from us the
graces of the spirit which we were clothed (with) in the (baptismal) pool. Moreover
also, from the time of the completion of the work one must be watchful, lest thieves,
by digging into the house, plunder everything which may be in the house; in like manner
also, when we receive the gifts of our Lord which are compared to possessions, it is
necessary to be continually watchful and vigilant in the night and in the day, with
virtuous and pure conduct; lest we having been found by Satan, who like a thief strays
and turns, in dissolute and unbecoming conduct of pleasure, he indeed cuts off the
strength of our buildings and enslaves our whole mind to his will; for which also the
Lord cautions us always to be watchful with good works, and therefore the instruction
of the teaching of our Lord is likened to a building. — [11] om.

    9.   [1] om. — [2] the. — [3] om. — [a] .or :worn — [4] is. — [5] you. — [6] has. — [7] he. — [8] + God.
— [b] lit. architect.

    9.   Lk 5:37,38.

them, they were new and were enduring the power of the new wine. ⌜But if [9] they shall grow old, they will not endure the power of the new wine. In like manner also, in the beginning of our creation we were new, handsome and becoming, in order to receive the instruction
5 of the teaching of God, on account of the innocence of childhood. And moreover after many years, as long as we shall be innocent of evil, we will be able to receive the power of the teaching as ⌜a child [10], as new leather bottles, which endure the power of the new wine. But if we are soiled and are worn out in the sensualities [c] of folly [11],
10 in the depriving [d] of greed, and in the drunkenness of indulgence, at that time beaten (and) spoiled, we are worn out in our sins and iniquities [12], thenceforth we are not able to receive the instruction of the teaching.

10. Also this is clear, that in our infancy, when God made us,
15 there was not in us, that which they supposed, for having departed they deprive us of life and [1] afterwards the works of evil are attached to us, as leather bottles that afterwards are worn out (and) grown old.
† And the Apostle bears witness to me when he says, ⌜he says [2] 'Be not children in your thoughts, but in evil be [a] children, for in your thoughts
20 you should be perfected' [b]. ⌜And when [3] we are [4] found innocent of evil, as at the beginning of our [5] creation [6], then we are able to receive the instruction of the teaching, ⌜and (are) [7] leather bottles that endure the power of the new wine, ⌜that (are) [8] in their newness;
⊙ as also the Prophet says, 'Why ⌜do they say, O [9] house of Israel, that
25 our sins and iniquities are in us and we in those same are worn out'. And the Prophet makes clear that our creation at the start was new, and [10] sin and [11] iniquities make (one) old and worn out.

11. Our Lord likened the instruction of his teaching to wine, ⌜and he indeed fulfilled the words of the Prophet [1], for [2] David says,

---

[9] And then. — [10] children.— [c] or : desires. — [11] + and. — [d] or : deprivation. — [12] + and.

10. [1] but. — [2] that. — [a] or : become. — [b] or : mature. — [3] that. — [4] may be. — [5] om. — [6] + and. — [7] read : 'as' B. — [8] del : om B. — [9] says the. — [10] + our. — [11] + our.

11. [1] om. — [2] as.

10. † I Cor 14:20. — ⊙ Ezk 33:10b.

'God [3] raises food from the earth and wine makes ⌜the heart of man [4] †
joyful'. And [5] as the Prophet said concerning [6] wine, ⌜that it is
that which [7] makes joyful, in like manner also the instruction of the
teaching of our Lord is our [8] rejoicer. For example, wine not only
makes the sorrowful joyful, but elevates the humble [9] and enriches 5
the poor, and indeed takes away cares and sorrows from all minds.
If anyone may be weak ⌜in strength [10] and shall drink wine, afterwards [11] he will forget the weakness ⌜of his strength because of the
wine drinking [12]. If giants may [13] fight with him, he will not at all
be afraid ⌜of them [14]. Also it is clear (that) if anyone drinks enough 10
wine and gets drunk, he will not care, nor be frightened, nor sorrow,
nor be sad. In like manner also, the instruction of the teaching of
our Lord, when we drink it and it is mixed with our minds, it strength-
ens our weakness, and we forget our lowness [15] and it indeed takes
away from us all cares and sorrows.   15

12. And more than all the words of wisdom, wine comforts the
⌜hearts of [1] mourners. ⌜For if you have sat down in order that you
may comfort those for whom there may be mourning and sorrow,
and pain and judgment, as much as you have pondered on (and) shall
compare the time with the sufferings which are before him, you will 20
awaken his mind to remember his loss. But if you will give him to
drink and intoxicate him, you remain silent (and) cease from him [a],
and the wine forgotten drives out from him all his misfortunes and
sorrows. And that which enflames his sufferings of his mind, which
had burned like the lighted lantern, the wine having ceased (and) 25
calmed extinguishes (it) and brings sleep. In like manner also we,
when the things of the world happen to us and we would seek comfort
on account of them and can not find (it) [2], when we shall turn to the
instruction of the teaching of our Lord, at that time little by little
it indeed [3] penetrates into our hearts [4]. And when we confess and 30

---

[3] om. — [4] om. — [5] om. — [6] that. — [7] om. — [8] a. — [9] thoughts. — [10] om. — [11] om. —
[12] and. — [13] om. — [14] om. — [15] iniquity.

12. [1] om. — [a] i.e. leave him alone. — [2] For the words make mention of the events
to him; but the wine (makes) joyful because he is silent and becomes calm and in sleep
he carries away all the cares of his sorrows; in like manner also we, when something
sorrowful happens in this world. — [3] om. — [4] minds.

11.   † Ps 104:14b-15a.

rejoice in it, thenceforth we are at rest (and) become calm, even [5] from all these things which were enflaming us. And [6] in that [7] way the instruction of the teaching of our Lord was likened to wine.

13. Moreover [1] why the instruction of the teaching of our Lord
5 was likened to wine, ⌐I shall say [2]. If ⌐it happens to a poor man seated [3] in the house of royalty to drink of the royal wine and he gets drunk, thenceforth [4] he will forget the house of his poverty. And the feet which are thirsty (and) [5] carried him ⌐to the royal house — when he enters (and) drinks [6] of the royal wine — ⌐his feet [7] ⌐do not
10 inquire [8] to carry him again [9] to ⌐the house of his poverty [10], ⌐for he drank wine and got drunk [11]. In like manner also, when we are called into the Church of our Lord, and we drink of his teaching and it enters (and) is mixed with ⌐our minds and thoughts [12], thenceforth we forget our previous home, and our feet do not inquire to carry us
15 to the house of our idolatry and to the road with which we came from heathenism [13], and [14] we turn [15] no more ⌐to it [16], for it was forgotten ⌐from our minds [17] because of our wine drinking.

† 14. And that which our Lord says, 'He who strikes [a] you on your [1] cheek, offer to him the other also [2]; and he who takes away [3]
20 your coat [b], give to him [4] your tunic [c]; he who [d] asks something [5] from you, do not withhold from him; and he who takes away ⌐something (of) yours [6], do not ask ⌐for that [7] from him', all this the intoxicated are able to do. For if we drink (and) get drunk and are submerged into the instruction of the teaching of our Lord, then [8] we are
25 able to do all this. For ⌐they abuse [9] the intoxicated and [10] he laughs, ⌐he is without and he asks not, they indeed take away whatever is his and he feels not, they laugh at him and he thinks nothing (about it). In like manner also, when we drink the instruction of the teaching of

---

5 om. — 6 om. — 7 this.

    13. 1 I shall say also moreover. — 2 om. — 3 a poor (man) shall happen to sit. —
4 om. — 5 om. — 6 to drink. — 7 om. — 8 are not disposed. — 9 om. — 10 his poor
house. — 11 om. — 12 our thoughts and minds. — 13 our heathen idolatry. — 14 om. —
15 return. — 16 om. — 17 om.

    14. a lit. gives you a slap. — 1 + other. — 2 om. — 3 + from you. — b i.e. outer
garment. — 4 + also. — c i.e. inner garment. — d or : whoever. — 5 om. — 6 om. —
7 om. — 8 om. — 9 if anyone abuses. — 10 or takes away his (things).

    14. † Lk 6:29,30.

our Lord who himself is that which makes joyful, and we get drunk
by it, thenceforth we are able to do all this which we heard. If
the idolatrous heathen who are debased, ruined (and) deprived of
the wine from this which we drank, shall laugh at and mock us, we
think nothing (about) their mockery on account of our drunkenness, 5
and if they slander us, it is nothing to us [11], we do not harbor resent-
ment and indignation. Even extreme suffering wine is able to make
(one) forget; for when [12] ⌜anyone is [13] condemned to death and [14]
they take him [15] away to be executed, they give him wine to drink
that he may be fearless and without pain. In like manner also, 10
when believers drink the instruction of the teaching of our Lord [16]
they get drunk. ⌜He is [17] condemned to death before the judges
and ⌜he dies [18] fearlessly; and they do not care about the fear and
dread of the judges, for they are intoxicated with the instruction
⌜of the teaching of our Lord [19]. Therefore the instruction of the 15
teaching of the [20] Lord is likened to wine.

15. Moreover the instruction of the teaching of our Lord is likened
to garments [1]. ⌜If it may be really true for us that our Lord truly
called his instruction 'garments' [2], ⌜(one) will know [3] that Moses
foretold (and) [4] indicated the garments [5] in the parables ⌜of the mys- 20
teries of this new teaching [6]. Moses made for Aaron and his sons
ephods and robes [a,7] and girdles and various new garements : and
he brought (and) placed them before God, that they may please him.
When the sons of Aaron transgressed the law, fire went out from
before [8] God and consumed them; and Moses said [b] to their tribe,
'Draw near! take them outside the camp'. And Moses says to Aaron, †
Eleazar (and) [9] Ithamar, 'Do not weep, lest you should soil [c] the ⊙
holy garments which you may have'. And [10] therefore our Lord
also likened his [11] teaching to garments. And in this manner the
instruction of our Lord is truly likened to new garments, and to the 30

[11] in like manner also when the idolatrous slander us, we laugh about them, and. —
[12] om. — [13] they who are. — [14] when. — [15] them. — [16] + and. — [17] they are. — [18] they
die. — [19] om. — [20] read : 'our' B.

15. [1] a garment; therefore he says, 'There is no one who takes a new piece of cloth
and puts (it) upon an old and worn garment'. — [2] certainly he writes for us his true
instruction in the name of a 'garment'. — [3] having known. — [4] and. — [5] garment. —
[6] in this new teaching of the mystery. For. — [a] or : cassock. — [7] + caps and mitres. —
[8] om. — [b] lit. says. — [9] and. — [c] or : abuse. — [10] om. — [11] the instruction of the.

15. † Lev 10 : 4b (Parphrase). — ⊙ Lev 10 : 6b ? (Paraphrase).

honorable and holy garment [12]. For every man who ⌜may be [13]
clothed with the ⌜garment of honor [14], there is praise and honor
and a great assembly [d] for him; on account of his [15] outer garment
they fear him, and his family respect him, and the tyrant masters
5 who raise laborers [e] and workmen in the course [f] of hostilities, do not
approach him because of respect for his [16] garments. In like manner
also, because we are clothed with the instruction of the teaching [17],
the Apostles are glad for us and the angels of heaven honor and praise
us, the hosts of demons flee from us, and sensualities are controlled [g]
10 by us.

16. And as garments prevent ⌜and keep [1] the cold and heat and
outrages ⌜from all who may be clothed with them [2], in like manner
also the instruction of the teaching of our Lord prevents and with-
holds from us all sicknesses and sorrows and outrages. ⌜Moreover
15 they who shall be clothed with the garment of honor and praise,
will be [a] spared in their garments; and they keep it from every stain
of contamination, for if the garments with which they shall be clothed
are offended [b] and are soiled, they also in fact will be laughed at and
mocked because disgraces and outrages reached their garments;
20 for if they offend and lose their garments, in the same moment their
honor and praise also are lost [3]. In like manner also [4], they who
⌜may be [5] clothed with the instruction of the teaching of our Lord,
if [6] they offend [c] and soil it, at that time also they will lose even [7] the
honor which they found by reason of the teaching of our Lord.

25 17. For if anyone may have outwardly, with words, put on the
teaching of our Lord, and in his heart he is bare of the good teaching,
he is likened to Nabath and Abiuth, the sons of Aaron, when they
were clothed with the holy garments, and without command they
dared according to their desires to offer the service of worship on the
30 altar, and they were burned with fire. In like manner also, they who
will take the name of our Lord outwardly and shall not do his will,
fall into severe punishment, because they soil the holy garments,
and they are indeed condemned. Moreover after the death of Nabath

---

[12] garments. — [13] is. — [14] honorable garment. — [d] or : public celebration. — [15] the. [e] i.e.
fieldworkers. — [f] lit. operation. — [16] the. — [17] + of our Lord. — [g] lit. obeys.

16. [1] om. — [2] om. — [a] lit. were (apodosis of conditional sentence). — [b] or : found
with fault. — [3] For if they who are clothed with honorable garments, soil them, they
will be laughed at. — [4] om. — [5] are. — [6] and. — [c] or : debase. — [7] om.

and Abiuth Moses gave the command ⌐to their brothers [1], that they must not weep and soil [a] their holy [2] garments. And as ⌐the sons of Aaron [3], while they were clothed with the holy [4] garments, their minds were found divided from the will (of God); when they died their [5] brothers took them and [6] they were taken away outside of the [5] camp; in this manner also we, when any doubt and works of corruption should appear in anyone [7], although he shall cover himself with the ⌐garment of the teaching [8], nevertheless after having died they [9] expel him [10] outside of the Church — ⌐they who were his beloved brothers — and when dead he is cast outside of the camp of life [11]. [10] Accordingly here the teaching of our Lord is likened to clothes, for we learn [12] by it. And it is likened to wine, for it was mixed with our minds; ⌐therefore it is not strange, for everything [13] whatever may be here, it is likened in many ways.

18. Moreover in ⌐all these [1] parables, our Lord fulfilled the Law [15] and the Prophets. The old and worn out clothes, as [2] we heard concerning the leather bottles, let us know that the old and worn out clothes also are [3] not old and worn out from the beginning, but when they are soiled and stained, then they become old and worn out. In like manner also, the teaching of our Lord which was sent to us [20] in order that we might be completely (and) perfectly clothed with it as with the garment of glory, and ⌐they renew [a], let us hold it [4]. But if we may be soiled [5], worn out and spoiled in our sins, ⌐though we intend to separate the teaching of our Lord and bring (it) back to this oldness which approached in us, nevertheless [6] ⌐there is no [25] agreement of the teaching of our Lord [7] with our oldness. ⌐Therefore our Lord says, 'There is no one who takes (and) tears a piece of cloth †from a new garment, and sews it upon an old and worn out garment' [8].

19. Moreover our Lord likened his teaching to fire, in that he says [1],

17. [1] om. — [a]. or: abuse — [2] om. — [3] om. — [4] om. — [5] (their). — [6] (and). — [7] us. — [8] teaching of the garment. — [9] add : 'remove (and)' B. — [10] him. — [11] om. — [12] read: 'are clothed' B. — [13] accordingly.

18. [1] the. — [2] + also. — [3] were. — [a] text is corrupt here, see Codex B. — [4] read : 'let us embrace it anew' B. — [5] + and. — [6] om. [7] the new teaching of our Lord does not agree. — [8] om (see Codex B p. 23).

19. [1] said.

18.   † Lk 5:36a.

† 'I came to cast fire upon the earth, and I wish that it were already kindled'. Moreover he also fulfilled this prophecy in the beginning. ⊙ God said ᵃ to Jeremiah ⌐the Prophet ², 'Thus says the Lord God of hosts, because you spoke this word, now behold I give my words 5 in your mouth, Jeremiah, as fire, and this people shall be as wood, and you ³ shall consume them'. Moreover Jeremiah himself says, ◓ 'I said ⁴ that I will remember no more the oracles of thy prophecy in my mouth, and in thy name on the house of Israel I will prophesy no more, and thy oracles in my mouth were as fire, for it is enflamed 10 and burns in all my bones; and I wished ⁵ to be calm (and) sober with my ⁶ prophecy in my heart, and I was not able to be patient ᵇ'.

20. And the Prophet made clear ⌐to us ¹ that ⌐this was ² by God Almighty ⌐by the Lord, that ³ his gifts ⌐should be ⁴ called fire. And Jesus came as ⁵ the fulfiller of the prophecy; he called his teachings 15 fire, ⌐that he might make clear that they are the same as the former prophecy. As Jeremiah made clear and showed concerning the fire which was burning and was enflamed in his heart and it was not harming him at all but was aiding him, others who were not doing the will of God, even the oracles, the fire which was the rejoicer and 20 helper of Jeremiah, was enflaming and was setting fire to them; in like manner also he called the oracles of our Lord a burning fire, for the fire does not enflame and set fire to the truth, nor gold and silver and precious stones, but to wood, grass (and) reeds, as also the Apostle says, for he became the fulfiller of the Gospel and prophecy. In this 25 manner the fire of our Lord dwells in our hearts and gives pleasure to us. If we shall be firm and true through faith, it does not set fire and enflame us but intoxicates and urges us to preach the way and to perfect it, as Jeremiah. And to them who were discouraged and empty, because the oracles of the prophecy of our Lord which they 30 hear and do them not were urging (them), those same oracles have become fire and they burn them ⁶.

— ᵃ lit. says. — ² om. — ³ it. — ⁴ spoke. — ⁵ wish. — ⁶ thy. — ᵇ or : endure.

20. ¹ om. — ² om. — ³ om. — ⁴ were. — ⁵ om. — ⁶ For as the oracles, the fire did not burn Jeremiah, but helped and strengthened and did not burn the truth; and the Lord says, 'I came to cast fire', which purifies and cleans his true preaching as true gold; and yet the same words when having become fire, burn, if anyone may have wood, grass (or) straw.

19.   † Lk 12:49. — ⊙ Jer 5:14. — ◓ Jer 20:9.

21.   Moreover the teaching of our Lord is likened to fire, for the
fire burns and flames only upward, because everything whatever
they cast downwards goes downward, but fire burns and flames only
upward. ⌜And enslaved, our minds are conducted to the heights
of heaven with love to our Lord, and when we receive the teaching 5
of our Lord, it burns and is enflamed as fire in our minds.   Moreover
the teaching of our Lord is likened to fire [1], for when ⌜it dwells in us
(and) [2] burns in our minds and is [3] enflamed in our bodies, it enflames
and burns from us all works of corruption, fornication, impurity,
idolatry, fraud, ⌜revenge, bitterness and [4] together with every evil. 10
And by that same fire we are perfected into beautiful vessels for use
as the divine ornament [5]; as [6] gold and silver ⌜that enters the fire
and the fire enflames and burns from it every impurity and rust, and
the gold and silver remain true [7].   In this manner [8] all works of
corruption are burnt from us by the fire of our Lord, and good works 15
remain for us.   They who become beautiful by fire [9] are perfected
in love, knowledge [10], mercy, humility and willingness.   And in this
way the teaching of our Lord is [11] likened to fire.   ⌜And in all this we
found that our Lord Jesus Christ confirmed prophecy and was following
the ways of the Prophets, and was fulfilling those same things [12].   20

22.   Moreover ⌜our Lord likened his word of life [1] to seeds, and
because [a,2] he likened to the ground which receives the seeds, ⌜in that
he says, 'Behold a sower went out to sow his seed, and when he sowed, †
there was that which fell on the road, was trampled [b] and the birds
gathered it; and there was that which fell on the rock, when it sprung 25
up, it immediately dried up because there was not moisture under
its roots; and there was that which fell among thorns, the thorns
grew up and choked it; and there was that which fell on good ground,
it sprung up, grew and gave fruit' [3].   And when he explained concerning [4] the saying, he says, 'That which fell on the road are those ⊙

21.   [1] read : 'In the same manner also, when we receive the teaching of our Lord, it
burns and is enflamed in our minds.   And enslaved, our minds are conducted to the
heights of heaven with love to our Lord' B. — [2] the fire. — [3] om. — [4] bitterness, revenge.
— [5] + and. — [6] + the corruption is burned from. — [7] and they remain beautiful. —
[8] + also. — [9] + and. — [10] read : 'pity' B. — [11] (is). — [12] om.
     22.   [1] the teaching of our Lord is likened to. — [a] text is corrupt here, see Codex B. —
[2] read : 'us' B. — [b] or : trodden underfoot. — [3] om. — [4] om.

22.   † Lk 8:5-8a. — ⊙ Lk 8:12-15.

who hear the word and [5] the devil comes (and) [6] takes away the word [7] from their hearts. And that which fell on the rocky place are those who when they hear ⌐the word [8], receive it [9] ⌐with joy [10] ⌐but because it has no roots in it [c], for a time they believe and in time of temptation
5 they fall away. And that which fell among the thorns are those who heard the word and in the cares of the world and the distraction [d] of riches and the pleasures [e] of folly they are choked, and they become unfruitful. And that which fell on fertile ground are those who with a pure heart and clean mind heard the word of truth, and they
10 became fruitful'. And he made clear and showed to us that he called the good men, good fertile ground [11].

23. ⌐Moreover also once more and in this manner also we found that he is the fulfiller of prophecy; for Jeremiah the Prophet says,
† 'Thus says the Lord God, to the house of the Judeans [1] and the inhabi-
15 tants of Jerusalem, choose for yourselves a good and fertile land, and sow not among the thorns; be purified before the Lord and remove the evil from your hearts, O house of Judah and inhabitants of Jeru- salem'. ⌐And this parable with which our Lord said that the good ground gives the fruit of life, the Prophet foretold and said, (that)
20 even where the thorns were, if the husbandman [a] takes courage, gathers (and) takes away the thorns, the seeds of life will live; for even the Prophet said that we are good and fertile ground, and the works of evil (are) thorns [2]. And this also [3] we ought to know, that the thorns are not from some other place, but (are) from him and from
25 the same thing as [4] the oldness of the garments and the leather bottles; and the weeds of the land are not from some other place, but (are) from contempt and idleness. ⌐In like manner also, all ground which destroys seeds, we find that it is from the idleness of the husbandman [b]; not that the ground itself is not able to cause the seeds which fell
30 on the road to live, for the ground on which the road was beaten hard

---

[5] + the bird — [6] and. — [7] seed. — [8] om. — [9] (it). — [10] om. — [c] lit. there are not for it roots in it. — [d] or : occupation. — [e] or : desires. — [11] and for want of roots, in the time of temptation they dry up; and the thorn, he called the pleasures of riches in the world which choke the teaching and they are made unfruitful; moreover he called the good men the good ground, which gave fruit.

23. [1] And in this manner he fulfilled the word of Jeremiah, when he said to the house of Israel. — [a] i.e. field-worker. — [2] om. — [3] om. — [4] + also. — [b] i.e. field- worker.

23. † Jer 4:3,4ab.

is itself by nature the same as all of the ground, and the seeds were trampled and destroyed because of the multitude of the trampling feet of passing men and animals [5].   In like manner also, we by our natures are good soil, in order to receive the seeds of the kingdom and to give the fruit of life, but if we will give our hearts to be an avenue [5] of the road for the words of strangers [6], then in that time, the good seeds which may be sown in us shall be trodden underfoot.

24.   ⌜And (as) always with these parables of nature and the creation in which God indeed established us, those things which are superfluous and additional kill us; like the seeds which may be on the road which [10] passed over the ground, are trampled, and it was deprived of its fruit [a], lest there be anyone who will think that the road did not pass over the prepared ground and injure it [1].   But [2] if a husbandman [b] shall be diligent, he [3] labors by day and watches by night, and he fences in his seeds and digs all around it a trench [4], he stays and [5] keeps it [6] [15] from strange hoofs.   ⌜And there are fruits of goodness in the watchful care of the diligent and steadfast husbandman.   For the husbandman knows that in no other way are there fruits of life for him, except by the seeds which may be sown by him.   In like manner we, if there is not life from anywhere else, except from the seed which we received [20] from the Gospel, as the Prophets witness to everything therein [7], let us close our ears to rebellious hearing and our hearts to vain useless thoughts, and let us not make our minds [8] a bridge for all the superstitious words ⌜to cross over [9]; and then we live.

25.   ⌜Our Lord spoke to us concerning the thorns; for as the thorns [25] do harm to the ground because they spring forth from it, in like manner sensualities are harmful for us.   And if anyone is able to show that the thorn is not from the ground, it is a possible thing for him to believe, that also the sensualities of evil are sent to us.   But as it is possible to gather (and) take away the thorns and for the seeds [30]

---

[5] Likewise the road is ground by nature and the trampling of passing men and animals killed the seeds. — [6] + witchcraft, astrology, divination, and vain things.

24.   [a] lit. its fruit was deprived. — [1] om. — [2] and. — [b] i.e. field-worker. — [3] one who. — [4] + and. — [5] (and). — [6] (it). — [7] There is good fruit for the diligent and steadfast husbandman.   But in no other way is there life except by the word which is sown in us. — [8] hearts. — [9] om.

† to live ¹, in like manner also ² the Prophet said ⌐to us, he says ³, 'Choose
for yourselves a good ⌐and fertile ⁴ land, and sow not among the
thorns, ⌐be pure before the Lord, and remove the evil from your
hearts, lest the wrath of the anger of the Lord shall have gone forth ⁵ as
⁵ fire and shall burn you ⁶, and there shall be no one who can extinguish
(it)'; for the thorn is food for the fire, and wheat (is) for the use of the
living. ⌐But if our works shall be wicked and painful as thorns, with
those same as with the thorns, we shall be burned in the fire. And
if we remove all wicked desires from our minds, thenceforth we will
¹⁰ dwell in good and fertile ground with the good seeds which we receive
and keep as wheat in the storehouse of life⁷.

26. ⌐As concerning the rock which our Lord spoke of, that those
who are on the rock flourish for a little time and quickly dry up, at
the time when I spoke about the glories of divinity, this name of
¹⁵ stone, with the weak seeds, this itself is chosen for the use of buildings.
And our Lord introduced this parable in order that it might make
clear that nothing in all creation is strange to him. Moreover why
are the seeds which may be on the rock weak ?¹ Because they
snatch (and) receive the first rain and there is no place of condensation
²⁰ in the earth for it, to enclose itself with the moisture of the water.
Moreover when the rays of the sun come (and) reach (it), they are
dispersed ᵃ not only on a rocky place but on all the ground. And
because there can not be moisture for it in the rocky place, it is moved
from the power of the sun, and all the seeds flourish ᵇ together, when
²⁵ that which dries up the seeds which may be on the rock ² shines on
them. ⌐In like manner also, we who heard the teaching of our Lord,
and enclosed (and) gathered it into our hearts, were as a good and
fertile ground which enclosed the moisture in itself ³; and they who
immediately snatch (and) receive the teaching as soon as they ⌐have
³⁰ opened (and) shall ⁴ read ⌐the Scriptures ⁵ before them, and ⁶ the

---

25. ¹ As the thorn grows in the ground, in like manner the thorn of sensuality is
sent into our wills; and as it is possible to gather the thorns and (for the seeds) to live
in the ground. — ² om. — ³ om. — ⁴ om. — ⁵ purify your hearts from evil lest the wrath
of God shall have gone forth. — ⁶ om. — ⁷ om.

26. ¹ moreover the seed on the rock. — ᵃ lit. loosened. — ᵇ lit. enjoy. — ² rocky
(place). — ³ om. — ⁴ om. — ⁵ om. — ⁶ om.

25. † Jer 4:3b,4ac.

truth of the teaching does not remain in their minds, they are likened
to the rocky ground; for the abundant waters are indeed upon it,
as also ⁷ upon all the ground, and it does not receive them; and when
any temptations reach (them) in the likeness of the sun, not only
on a man who ⌐may have ⁸ resembled the rock, do they reach, ⌐but ₅
on every man ⁹.

27.　　Moreover they who kept ¹ the truth of the teaching in their
minds ², remember that our Lord is ³ the Son of God; he was persecuted, imprisoned, tortured, hungered, despised and ⁴ molested, and
he taught us the same thing; and as long as we remember this, we ₁₀
rejoice, and grow and ⁵ are nourished in our temptations, as seeds
flourish through drinking water, ⌐and it ⁶ keeps them, and ⁷ they
are not ⁸ moved from before the sun.　Moreover they who receive
the teaching as a cure for temporary benefit, when any temptation
overtakes them, they ⌐are considered superficial ᵃ,⁹.　And in this ₁₅
manner the faith of our Lord is likened to seeds.

28.　　Moreover our Lord likened his faith to a grain of mustard-seed,
in that ⌐our Lord ¹ says, 'To what is the Kingdom of Heaven like, †
or to what resemblance do I liken it ²?　It is likened to a grain of
mustard-seed, which when ³ a man took, he sowed it ⁴ in the ⁵ garden, ₂₀
and ⁶ it grew (and) became larger and arose like a tree and the birds
of the air ᵃ dwelt in its branches'.　⌐And in that same oracle he says,
'The Kingdom of Heaven is like leaven, which a woman took and ⊙
mixed it in three bushels of meal ᵇ, until all ᶜ the dough was leavened ᵈ'.
And for that reason let us know that with every one of its aspects, ₂₅
our faith is likened to the forms of all things ⁷; because ⁸ a grain of
mustard-seed is not like leaven ⌐in its appearance ⁹, and the kingdom
of God, ⌐he says ¹⁰, is like both in its effect.　He likened it to a grain of

---

⁷ om. — ⁸ has. — ⁹ om.

27.　¹ keep. — ² hearts. — ³ (is). — ⁴ om. — ⁵ (and) we. — ⁶ which. — ⁷ when. —
⁸ om. — ᵃ lit. on the face. (text is corrupt here, see Codex B). — ⁹ read : 'wither before it'
B.

28.　¹ he. — ² + as. — ³ del : om B. — ⁴ del : om B. — ⁵ read : 'his' B. — ⁶ om. —
ᵃ or : heavens. — ᵇ or : flour. — ᶜ or : whole. — ᵈ This quotation is from Mt in spite of
the preceding statement. — ⁷ For he shall make clear that all our faith is likened in
many ways. — ⁸ om. — ⁹ which a woman took and hid in the dough, until the whole
was leavened, nevertheless it is compared to faith in one aspect here. — ¹⁰ om.

28.　† Lk 13:18,19. — ⊙ Mt 13:33.

mustard-seed which having ⌈risen like a tree (and) grown large [11],
becomes a repose for the birds of the air.   Because our Lord came,
appeared to us a man short of stature, ignoble, despised and humble,
died and was buried as a stranger, arose [e] through divinity, and [12]
5 appeared with glory, and [13] became the ⌈rest and peace [14] of all man-
kind, which ⌈we have [15] compared to the birds, therefore our form
has come forth from above, and with our minds and faith we took
flight and [16] soared and ascended from all the distractions of the [17]
world, and from all [18] the evil thoughts; and ⌈moreover from the
10 same place we [19] knew that our habitation is in heaven, whence [20]
we expect the Savior, our Lord Jesus Christ.

   29.   Moreover the faith of our Lord is like [1] a grain of mustard-seed
which grew (and) grew large and [2] arose like a tree; because it is sown
and dwells in us first as something little [a], and [3] little by little it grows
15 and takes root and its roots are established in our minds; for at first
we [4] desire only this, to believe in God; and then afterwards when [5]
faith [6] becomes established in us, thenceforth we separate from our
fathers, and forgotten we depart from our mothers, and we detach
ourselves from our family [b], and we do not intermingle with our
20 friends ⌈who (are) [7] of the world, and we are ⌈cut from [8] all our conduct
which (is) of the world, because the faith which we received previously
as something little [c], as a grain of mustard-seed, conquers us completely [9].   If our Lord himself is [10] the seed like a grain of mustard-
seed, and his [11] Father sowed him into the world, as in a garden,
25 for the world is of the Father, and if ⌈the faith [12] of our Lord ⌈is
compared [13] to a grain of mustard-seed, and it was sown in us, we
will know that in fact we were his, for the sower sowed in his garden.

   30.   And it is likened to leaven; for leaven is one that draws [1]
and takes captive, and it always has this power [2]; when it is mixed
30 with all [3] the dough, it changes ⌈and draws [4] all the dough into its
form of being; and the leaven never turns (and) becomes flour.   In like
manner also, the Kingdom of God was likened to leaven, because it

---

[11] grown (and) risen like a tree. — [e] or : came back to life again. — [12] om. — [13] om. —
[14] peace and rest. — [15] are. — [16] (and). — [17] this. — [18] om. — [19] read : 'we already' B. —
[20] + also.

   29.   [1] likened to. — [2] (and) arose (and). — [a] lit. with littleness. — [3] + then. — [4] I. —
[5] om. — [6] our faith. — [b] or : kindred. — [7] om. — [8] finished with. — [c] lit. with littleness.
— [9] add : 'And' B. — [10] (is). — [11] the. — [12] we believe. — [13] he was compared.

   30.   [1] add : 'and takes away' B. — [2] add : 'in itself' B. — [3] del : om B. — [4] om.

is mixed in us in body and [5] soul and spirit [a] in the likeness of the
three bushels of dough; and it is never sown into our [6] humanity in
order ⌐for this [7] to become like us [8], but in that [9] manner only, because
it is made [b],[10] in us and ⌐draws and takes captive and changes [11] all
of us into divinity, after the fashion of leaven.   And as leaven, which [12]   5
at first mixes itself with the flour [c] and together [d] they become like
the dough when [13] unleavened, but the power of the leaven having [14]
hidden in the dough in an invisible manner and having taken captive
much dough little by little, acts in the leaven which in appearance
was [15] smaller than the dough, and [16] turns it [17] (the dough) to itself,   10
and thenceforth [18] the dough is ⌐no longer [19] separated from the leaven,
because it was absorbed [e],[20]; in this manner the divinity of Christ
came, (and) was mixed with [21] our humanity; and Christ became
like us, and he was mixed with [22] our dough; and it did not appear
that he was not mortal [f], as leaven is not apparent from the dough   15
when it is mixed; and little by little ⌐they enter [23] ⌐by the power of
Christ in secret.   And as leaven, we were drawn and were mixed [24]
with his divinity, as also he was mixed with our humanity, and no
longer are we separated from him, ⌐for we were [25] absorbed into him.
And in the same manner is the saying which the Apostle spoke, ⌐he   20
says [26], 'Death was submerged [g] by life'.   ⌐In this manner the King-   †
dom of our Lord (is) likened to leaven [27].

     31.   ⌐Moreover also let us know this, that if you would like to
mix leaven with something else, it does not receive nor mix with
gold nor pearls, which are exalted and glorious [1]; nor with dung,   25
for it ⌐appears repulsive [2]; nor with iron, which is hard ⌐and solid [3],
nor with wool and silk, which are fine and delicate; ⌐and with something else which is mixed and becomes useful [4]; and there is not

---

[5] om. — [a] lit. breath. — [6] om. — [7] om. — [8] man. — [9] this. — [b] text is corrupt here,
see Codex B. — [10] read : 'mixed' B. — [11] changes, draws, (and) takes captive. — [12] om. —
[c] or : meal. — [d] lit. with it. — [13] om. — [14] has. — [15] seemed. — [16] om. — [17] (it). — [18] om.
— [19] not. — [e] lit. submerged. — [20] + into it. — [21] into. — [22] in. — [f] lit. man. — [23] read :
'he enters' B. — [24] read : 'into the dough. Now Christ is hid in us like leaven and we
are drawn and are mixed' B. — [25] read : 'for we shall be' B. — [26] om. — [g] or : absorbed. —
[27] om.

     31.   [1] Moreover leaven does not mix with gold nor pearls, which are precious. —
[2] offends. — [3] om. — [4] om.

     30.   † I Cor 15:54c + II Cor 5:4c.

another thing which turns and becomes leaven, except flour ^a ⌐and leaven, which are consolidated and are united ⁵ with one another. In like manner also, the Kingdom of Heaven is ⁶ confirmed ⌐and united ^{b,7} with us, and we are ⁸ confirmed in order to receive it, and
5 ⌐we shall be separated from it no more ⁹. Altogether we were to know that we ought to receive ¹⁰ it, as the stone for the building, and as ¹¹ the ground for the seeds, and as a garden for herbs, and as ¹² flour ^c for the leaven, and as ¹³ the vineyard for the plants, and ¹⁴ as leather bottles for wine, as garments for a piece of cloth. Therefore
10 as all these things which our Lord showed us ¹⁵ by parables that they are proper to each other in whatever (way) they are confirmed; in like manner also we were confirmed in order to receive this ¹⁶ kingdom ⌐which was sent to us ¹⁷, and the kingdom itself was confirmed, that ⌐he might send (it) ¹⁸ to us.
15   32. Moreover our Lord likened his faith to silver, in that he says,
† 'A noble man went to a distant land to receive the crown ^a of a kingdom and to return. He called his ten servants, and gave them each a talent ^b, and he says to them, Let out on hire (and) employ that until I come'. But it is proper for me to say that Jesus is the noble and
20 rich man; because I ¹ have believed that by nature of divinity he is ⌐the one who is ² the great, high, transcendent, glorious, rich person ⌐and Lord of all natures ^c, who appears and who does not appear, and (is) the creator (and) decorator of all natures, visible and invisible ³. Moreover ⌐(he was) a noble man ⁴, because he was ⁵ from the tribe
25 of Judah. Accordingly ⁶, there were kings and prophets ⌐from it ⁷. Although ⁸ ⌐there were other ⁹ wise men, ⌐nevertheless in behalf
⊙ of Solomon it is written in the Book of Kings that ¹⁰, ⌐'Not to anyone ¹¹ previous to him ⌐was given such wisdom ¹², nor since ⌐him was given to anyone ¹³'. And ⌐although there were other kings, nevertheless
30 on David was put the testament with oaths concerning the kingdom ¹⁴,

---

^a or : meal. — ⁵ which are mixed. — ⁶ was. — ^b lit. mixed. — ⁷ in order to mix. — ⁸ were. — ⁹ to turn and become like it. — ¹⁰ have. — ¹¹ om. — ¹² om. — ^c or : meal. — ¹³ om. — ¹⁴ om. — ¹⁵ om. — ¹⁶ om. — ¹⁷ om. — ¹⁸ it might be sent.

32.   ^a or : authority. — ^b or : mina. — ¹ we. — ² om. — ^c or : essences. — ³ for all of him is confirmed. — ⁴ he is great. — ⁵ is. — ⁶ from which. — ⁷ om. — ⁸ and. — ⁹ om. — ¹⁰ as Solomon who. — ¹¹ no one. — ¹² om. — ¹³ was. — ¹⁴ he confirmed his testament of the oath on David.

32.   † Lk 19:12,13. — ⊙ Allusion to I Kg 3:12.

as also Jeremiah ⌐the Prophet [15] says, 'If it may be possible for you ☻
to interrupt the day and the night from [d] their (proper) time, then
also my oath ⌐which I swore to David my servant may be interrupted [16],
⌐for him to have [17] a son [18] who shall sit on the throne of his kingdom'.
⌐And it appears that our Lord with his divinity and with his humanity 5
is noble [19]. ⌐Moreover they who think that Christ is from another
nature, and from God nothing was established by him, and deny
him human nobility, it is not right for them to call him noble [20].

33.   And our Lord likened his faith to silver. ⌐Moreover in The
Wisdom of Solomon it is written, it says [1], 'A gold apple on a silver †
tray [2], things of reproach to obedient ears'. ⌐And our Lord made
clear to us that his words are equivalent to the writings which they
preached before him.

34.   Moreover the faith of our Lord is like engraved silver, which
is counted at the rendering of accounts; for ⌐every man who has 15
silver in his hand [1], everything [2] is found ⌐before him because of the
silver [3] : wheat [4], wine, ⌐garments and food, and everything which
may be necessary [5] to life and to the necessities of man. In like
manner also, when we possess [6] faith, ⌐thenceforth by means of it [7]
we are able to fast, to love the brethren, to give gifts [a], to be persecuted, 20
and to be patient in all desires; ⌐as a believer we know that our wages
of compensation remain [b] for us in heaven. As when our Lord was
here, to everyone whoever approached him concerning all pains and
sicknesses [8], ⌐in this manner he spoke to each of them [9], 'Your faith †
saved you'. ⌐Moreover when the Apostles possessed faith, then by 25
means of it they began to cast out demons, to cleanse the leprous,
to raise the dead, and to give new life to men in heavenly places [10].

---

[15] om. — [d] lit. at. — [16] om. — [17] to give to him. — [18] man. — [19] A great man and a
noble Christ. — [20] om.
    33.   [1] As also Solomon in (the Book) of Wisdom says. — [2] table.
    34.   [1] om. — [2] + with silver. — [3] om. — [4] + and. — [5] and that which is necessary. —
[6] keep. — [7] om. — [a] i.e. tithes and offerings. — [b] lit. rest. — [8] om. — [9] as also our Lord
when he healed the sick, said. — [10] After which the disciples also by faith began to raise
the dead and heal the sick and cleanse the leprous, and etc.

    32.   ☻ Jer 33:20,21.
    33.   † Prov 25:11b,12b.
    34.   † Lk 7:50b.

35.   ⌜And in this manner faith is likened to silver; for as everything which may be necessary to life in this world is purchased with silver, in like manner all things whichever may be necessary for the (coming) life are purchased with faith.   Also because of that, love, which the
5 Apostle values more than all, when we believe we are able to purchase it with faith ¹.   Therefore ⌜our faith ² is likened to silver, for silver is able to satisfy all the necessities of those who may have it; that (is) (silver) which shall have the stamp of the image ³ of the lord of the land, that it might circulate through it (i.e. the land) which is under
10 his command.   But if anyone shall go to a foreign land ᵃ and shall have silver engraved with the stamp of the image of a different ᵇ king, and shall not have a letter for the lord of the ⁴ land, he will be in ⌜very much ⁵ trouble, for even ⁶ the poor borrowers will not receive from him ⌜that which is not useful to them; because not even the
15 merchants receive that by which they do not profit.   Although clothes and food and all necessary things are found in abundance, nevertheless he is caused to suffer famine and cold and he dies, because the silver he has in (his) hand (was) scorned (and) rejected ⁷.

36.   Moreover when our Lord ⌜preached to us this faith which
20 he likened to silver, he spoke with frankness of his servants, he says ¹,
† 'You shall employ that until I come' ²; because he knew that the true stamp of the image of the lord of the land is on it, and it is honored by all persons.   Even here there is that which is like his which he brought, for upon his arrival he demanded with interest.   But if the
25 silver is ³ in the same manner in which it came, there shall not be any interest for him, and from where is the interest given ?   Or why does Marcion say that his way ⌜is not likened to things ⁴ ?   When he came, he who had one talent, that is, he who is like Marcion and the other sects, and the rich (man) ⌜was (there) ⁵ for the one who had

---

35.   ¹ For as all things of necessity in this world are bought with silver, in like manner also all (things) for life in the (other) world are accomplished with faith. — ² the faith of our Lord. — ³ + of the writing. — ᵃ or: shall become a foreigner. — ᵇ or another. — ⁴ its. — ⁵ great. — ⁶ om. — ⁷ and a merchant does not receive that which is not of use to him. From famine and from the cold he dies, although there may be much clothing and food in that land; they do not receive (the silver).

36.   ¹ distributed the silver to his servants, he says with frankness. — ² shall come. — ³ (is). — ⁴ shall not be (like) things. — ⁵ came.

36.   † Lk 19:13c.

one talent to give an answer, and [6] instead of having [7] stood and
said with a brazen-face, 'I was afraid of you, because you were [8] a ⊙
severe man, and therefore I did not lend your silver', he ought to
have said that 'the borrowers did not take it from me; I intended
to find something similar, and I did not find (it) in order to increase [5]
it'.

37. Moreover because the silver which came ⌜to this world [1]
of [2] our Lord was honored (and) [3] was acceptable, and they who
received it added to it, each [4] as much as he was able to gather, there
was [5] he who (had) ten doubled and there was [6] he who (had) five. [10]
⌜And in fact this same silver which was gathered in this present life,
was honored in celestial regions, and it was clear that there is one Lord
with these two natures, above and below, and on account of his decree
(there is) one issue of silver, (and) this is in circulation in all regions
and is honored [7]. ⌜And in this way his faith is likened to silver. [15]
And with these parables with which our Lord said that the Kingdom
of Heaven is like everything; because he likened it, he made clear
and showed us how the Kingdom shall be, and it was likened to various
things, as [8] it is easy for him ⌜to decrease and to increase, to grow poor,
to grow rich, to die and to live, and all that which he is able to do [9]. [20]

38. And moreover this parable that our [1] Lord said, he says,
'A noble man went [2] to a distant land to receive a [3] kingdom and †
to return' [4], made clear to us that ⌜the habitation of the Kingdom and
its nature are [5] above, and thence it comes here, on account of this
our Lord was here with us. And indeed he was true man, for he [25]
clothed himself with humanity, ⌜and he was noble; for that reason
that which (is) above was written [6]. ⌜And for that reason he says [7],
'To receive the crown of a kingdom and to return', for when he comes ⊙
with his formidable and glorious arrival [8], the king [9] comes ⌜and

---

[6] om. — [7] read : 'that which he' B. — [8] read : 'are' B.

37. [1] in this manner. — [2] with. — [3] and. — [4] om. — [5] is. — [6] is. — [7] om. — [8] In this
manner the faith of our Lord is likened to silver, for having received the silver from
us he rendered (it) celestial; and he likened the Kingdom of heaven to various things,
for everything. — [9] om.

38. [1] the. — [2] traveled. — [3] the crown of a. — [4] + and. — [5] the kingdom by its
nature and being is. — [6] om. — [7] moreover. — [8] + for. — [9] judge.

36. ⊙ Lk 19:21a.
38. † Lk 9:12. — ⊙ Lk 9:12.

God and the judgment and the sentence of death and life, of rejoicing and suffering, when he shall sit on the throne of terrible fear and encouragement, as the hosts of angels shall stand before his face with fear and dread. Therefore (as) true man he departed from us; as king he is for us, for the head of the Kingdom and of the divinity is above [10]. But it is [11] clear to every man, as [12] it is proper for a king to become and be called a king ⌐in this manner [13], when he shall have [a] cities and [14] villages and [15] crops, treasures, troops [16], executioners, deputies, attendants, couriers, throne guards, and [17] chamber guards and [18] all the services of the kingdom, ⌐which clearly appear before his eyes. But if the king should go all alone, and he should be in a desolate place, when all these services will be far from him, he is not a king, or who shall there be that can call him a king, when he shall be alone and there shall be no one with him [19].

39. Therefore truly indeed [1] our God is the great king, whose are the heavens and the earth, the ⌐angelic archangels [2] and stars and [3] death and life, principalities and powers, lightning and thunder, ⌐heights and depths [4], and all created things which appear and which do not appear [5]. He is the king and the Lord of all natures [a] and on account of the image of the form of man which Christ was clothed with by [6] the Father in the heights, thus he himself is the king, who [7] said that he goes forth (and) receives his [8] ⌐kingdom and returns [9]. And those who reject the humanity of Christ, how can they think that he went forth to receive the [10] kingdom from a place which can not exist? But ⌐if there may be some who might think that at one time he had dwelt without angels, principalities and powers, and he had nothing, over whom was he even called a king, this one who was without possessions until he came here? And if he acquired the kingdom from men who are created here by the true king, wherefore they said, 'Christ made his angels, principalities and powers, and he was called king over them'; it was clear that certainly he did

---

[10] in terror and suffering, and glory when he sits on the glorious throne. — [11] + also. — [12] read : 'that' B. — [13] om. — [a] lit. when that there shall be to him. — [14] om. — [15] om. — [16] services. — [17] om. — [18] om. — [19] and when a king shall not have these, how shall he be king ?

39. [1] and rightly. — [2] angels. — [3] om. — [4] depths and heights. — [5] add : 'And' B. — [a] or : essences. — [6] which he received from. — [7] he. — [8] a. — [9] the crown of a kingdom and come. — [10] crown of a.

not become king [b], except by the true king who is Lord of all natures.
For behold Christ when the sects of heretics intended to alienate him;
it is clear that he acquired his possessions here in the creation of
the great and wealthy king, and he was called king over it [11].

40. ⌜And our Lord called the city his glorious habitation; in that [1] 5
he gave ten cities of authority to him who gained ten talents; and
five cities to him who gained five talents. ⌜Moreover in fact [2] in the
beginning (of this parable) ⌜it is [3] written, ⌜it says [4], he called his ten
servants [5]. And when he came at his arrival, ⌜and they came to
give (their) accounts, only three are written who came [6], and it spoke 10
not to us concerning the seven, what happened to them, nor [7] why
they did not come. ⌜But since it is written, it says, that [8] he called
his ten servants, he spoke (this) in order to fulfill the whole number
of the discipleship; as also in fact from the beginning, God established
the number ten ⌜in order to number [9] all the peoples [a] : the Greeks [10], 15
Romans [11], Syrians [12], Parthians, and [13] he who counts all the numbers
up to ten, also returns to (the number) one ⌜in order to add on to [14]
the tenth number. Moreover God abundantly showed to us his
patience and indignation in the tenth number; for to the tenth generation God forgave through his patience the first iniquity of man, 20
and then he brought the flood upon them, and ⌜then he showed [15]
only Noah, for he was just. Moreover God [16] purified the children
of Noah to the tenth generation, and raised Abraham. And in Sodom
if there had been found ten righteous (people), ⌜says the Lord [17],
it would have escaped from the destruction [18]. And God [19] punished 25
the unjust (and) guilty Egyptians with ⌜a rod of ten plagues [20], and
he added no more. In like manner also, our Lord introduced the
tenth number in [21] the first example which he ⌜has set [22], and the
total of all the number of the discipleship, he called ten.

41. And moreover they all appeared [1] in three forms; the one 30
with ten talents interest [a,2], the one [3] with five and the other one
without interest; that one who had [4] ten talents received authority

---

[b] or : reign. — [11] he is Lord of all.

40. [1] om. — [2] But why. — [3] is it. — [4] that. — [5] servants. — [6] it is written that only
three came to give (their) accounts. — [7] or. — [8] Because he says. — [9] (and) has numbered.
— [a] lit. languages. — [10] + and. — [11] + and Armenians, and. — [12] + and. — [13] moreover. — [14] he adds. — [15] read : 'he saved' B. — [16] he. — [17] om. — [18] wrath. — [19] he. —
[20] ten rods. — [21] according to. — [22] had been.

41. [1] came. — [a] lit. hire, wages. — [2] + and. — [3] other. — [4] added.

(over) ten cities. He gained ten talents because he did and fulfilled
every command; for every command [5] which our Lord gave us, was
compared to ten talents. And this other [b,6] one who came with ten
talents [7] interest [8], because he did and fulfilled all the commands, even
5 to this one are compared, all those who heard and did and fulfilled
what ever was commanded of them. And the other one who came
with five talents interest, ⌐because he [9] did half of the command which
he heard, and half he did not do, ⌐even to this one are compared,
all those who heard the command of life, and they accosted the prac-
10 tice [c] of our way (of life), and were not able to fulfill (it) [10]. And the
other one also [11] who came without interest, even to him are compared,
all those who heard the ⌐word of life [12] and did not accost its practice.

42. ⌐And all the disciples who are compared to the number who
fulfilled to the tenth, come in three forms. They come from them,
15 when the whole shall be done and fulfilled; and they come from them,
when the half shall be done, and half not done; and they come from
them, when the half of the half shall be done; and they come from
them, when absolutely nothing shall be done [1]. ⌐That one by whom
the whole shall be done and fulfilled, he comes with joy, (and) stands
† before the Lord and says, 'Lord, ⌐thy talents [2] gained ten talents [3]';
and he [4] received authority (over) ten cities, ⌐because he did and
fulfilled the whole; (and) [5] he received all unfailing glories, and the
glories which he (the Lord) gave ⌐to him [6] were called, ten cities,
because (he had) fulfilled to the tenth. And that one who gained
25 five talents, received authority (over) five cities, for ⌐this one [7] receives
half as much glory as the first one, in the world of life, and his pay [a]
was called, five cities, as half of the tenth number; as the Apostle
⊙ says, 'Each man [8] according to his labor ⌐receives his wages' [9]. Moreover ⌐the one [10] who came ⌐without pay [b,11], his [12] lord called him,
unbeliever, because he believed not and did not gain; for he who

---

[5] teaching. — [b] text is corrupt here, see Codex B. — [6] del : om B. — [7] + showed. —
[8] addition. — [9] that one who. — [c] lit. work. — [10] om. — [11] om. — [12] command.

42. [1] Now by this he made clear that the disciples who come, some have fulfilled
the whole and some half of the command, and some none. — [2] the talents which. —
[3] om. — [4] + did (and). — [5] it is clear that. — [6] om. — [7] he. — [a] or : salary (lit. gift). —
[8] om. — [9] received wages. — [10] he. — [b] or : wages. — [11] empty. — [12] the.

42. † Lk 19:16b. — ⊙ I Cor 3:8b.

believes that there is payment [c] for good [13] works, in that time also [14]
he begins to work. And ⌈if we would teach other men, when we
induce them to believe in the faith, we should also commend to them
the Word of our Lord [15]. And because he did not believe in one of
these forms, even the name of faith which he has, is taken away from 5
him in the end, and then he is cast to extermination and to perdition [d].
For everyone who is condemned to death, at first they strip [e] him
and then they execute [f] (him). In like manner also, this one who
shall have taken only the name of faith, who is compared to silver and
garments, and did not accost its practice, the name of faith which 10
was called talent, is taken away from him, ⌈and then he is condemned [16].

43. Since our Lord called his glorious habitation [a] the city, truly
the faith of our Lord is likened to cities; because the king may give
the authority over cities and villages to anyone [1] of his [2] servants. 15
And the servant resides in the palace of the king, and washes himself
in his bathing tubs [b] and he sits on the throne of his kingdom and
he strolls on his walks. And in this only is the servant-ruler smaller
than the great king, that he is his lord, and he knows that he himself
is not the head, ⌈and the authority he has over his dominion (is) from 20
his lord. In like manner also, when our Lord renders to us the compassion of his mercy, and draws us to himself and to his place, we
dwell in his paradise [c] and we indeed become delicate [d] in his light,
and become joyful in his goodnesses, and we share in and partake of
all his possessions [3], with the exception of this (that) we ⌈shall be 25
smaller than he [4], for he ⌈shall be the [5] head, and we receive from him
the privilege [e] to enjoy his gifts [f]. ⌈And the faith of our Lord is
likened to this [6].

44. It is written in the Gospels, that our Lord likened his faith
to plants [1], it says, 'A man planted his [2] vineyard; he encircled and †

c or : compensation. — [13] om. — [14] om. — [15] when we obtain through instruction the
things in faith, we are paid it when the Lord teaches it. — [d] or : destruction. — [e] lit.
plunder. — [f] lit. kill. — [16] om.

43.   [a] lit. habitation of his glory. — [1] one. — [2] the. — [b] or : pools. — [c] lit. Kingdom. —
[d] or : nice (lit. soft). — [3] in like manner also we, for we go up and enjoy of the glory of
his Kingdom, and of the delicacies of his possessions. — [4] we are small. — [5] is our. —
[e] or : right. — [f] or : grace. — [6] om.

44.   [1] a plant. — [2] om.

44.   † Mk 12:1b.

closed it with a wall; he prepared ³ a wine-press vat ᵃ in it, and indeed ⁴
built a tower ⌜in it ⁵'. ⌜And in the same oracle he makes clear that
he indeed worked in the vineyard until the time for fruit, and the
laborers ᵇ denied him ⁶. And moreover ⁷ in another place it says,
⊙ 'I am the vineyard ⁸ and you ⌜are the vines ⁹, ⌜every vine which
in me may be planted and does not give fruit, is taken away ᶜ'¹⁰'.
⌜For although this is hidden from the Gospels which the strange
Marcionites read, nevertheless from that which is written by the
Apostle, there is proof for them that this was truly written in the
10 Gospels, that we are compared to plants; and the Marcionites erased
◓ this. The Apostle writes in the letter to the Romans, he says, 'For
if we have been planted together in the death of our Lord, in like
manner also in his resurrection'. And moreover it is written in the
first letter to the Corinthians, that they are plants of God, it says ¹¹,
⚶ 'I planted, Apollos watered, but God gave the growth ᵈ'.

45. And with these parables the ¹ Scriptures fulfilled the teaching
of prophecy. Isaiah the Prophet says that men who have believed
are plants of life, and when they ⌜had become ² void of the works ³
† of life, thenceforth they become a desolate vineyard, he says, 'I planted
20 a vineyard in a favorite ⁴ place, ⌜in a fertile place; I enclosed (it)
with a fence and strongly ᵃ circled (it) with a wall; I planted new
plants, I cleaned, I pruned, I cultivated ᵇ, I adorned (it) with arbors;
I built a tower, I made a wine-press vat ᶜ; I expected ᵈ that it would
bring forth ᵉ grapes for me, (and) it brought forth thorns and thistles.
25 Now, men of Judah and inhabitants of Jerusalem, do justice between
me and my vineyard. What was there still to do to my vineyard,

---

³ digged. — ᵃ lit. a ditch by the wine-presses — ⁴ om. — ⁵ om. — ᵇ i.e. field-workers. —
⁶ om. — ⁷ om. — ⁸ vine. — ⁹ (are) the branches. — ᶜ lit. pulled up. — ¹⁰ om. — ¹¹ Since
this is written in the Gospels and the Marcionites cut and concealed (it) from the Gospels,
the Apostle bears witness that it was written, and the Marcionites erased this; it is decla-
red in the letter to the Romans that we are compared to a plant, 'For if we have been
planted together in the likeness of his death, in like manner also shall we be in his
resurrection'; in the letter to the Corinthians. — ᵈ lit. made to grow.

45. ¹ our. — ² read : 'become' B. — ³ read : 'work' B. — ⁴ read : 'visible' (or : 'high') B.
— ᵃ lit. with strength. — ᵇ lit. made soft. — ᶜ lit. a ditch by the wine-press. — ᵈ or :
waited. — ᵉ lit. come (and) bring.

44. ⊙ Jn 15:5a,2a. — ◓ Rom 6:5. — ⚶ I Cor 3:6.
45. † Isa 5:1b-7.

and I did not do (that) for it ?   I expected that it would bring forth [f] grapes for me, (and) it brought forth [g] thorns and thistles for me. Now I personally will tell what I will do to my vineyard : I will break down the solidness [h] of the fence and it shall be for plundering, I shall destroy and trample the walls with armies; I will abandon my vine- [5] yard, for it shall not be pruned and cleaned nor shall it be cultivated ; thorns shall sprout out and add to it as in the wasteland; I shall command my clouds, that they shall not shower on my vineyard ; for the vineyard of the Almighty is the House of Israel, and the men of Judah a beloved [i] new plant; I expected that I would find in it [10] justice and injustice was found [j]; I expected righteousness and there was deprivation [k,5]'.

46.   And after ⌐the desolation of [1] this vineyard, concerning which he said that he himself is the House of Israel, God makes the desolate mountains (to be) with seeds and plants. Isaiah says [2], 'It shall † happen in that day ⌐(that) every place in which [3] there shall be a thousand measures [a] of the vineyard at [b] a thousand thousand [c] measures [d], shall become wasteland and shall return to thorns.   And [4] many skillful archers shall descend [e] into (it) [5], for all the land shall become wasteland and full of thorns.   And every mountain which [20] shall not be plowed up (and) furrowed, no one shall go [f] there (for) fear, ⌐for there shall become [6] from the wasteland and ⌐thorny place [7], pasture for the lamb and trampling for the ox [8]'. As concerning the vineyard, the Prophet explained and showed us that it is not the vineyard, but ⌐the goodness of [9] the House of Israel ⌐(which) is called [25] the desirable vineyard, and the faith of God was planted in them as a newly planted vineyard [10], and when they returned to idolatry they became desolate mountains, (and) [11] produced in them evil works as thorns; in like manner also, we were desolate mountains, for we

---

[f] lit. come (and) bring. — [g] lit. came (and) brought. — [h] or : strength. — [i] or : favorite. — [j] or : appeared. — [k] or : injustice (lit. degradation). — [5] and fertile (place); I digged, I pruned, I cultivated, and etc.; because it did not produce fruit, I indeed abandoned (it), he says, and it became trampled by armies, and it shall not be cleaned and pruned.

46.   [1] om. — [2] add : 'And' B. — [3] where. — [a] lit. palm of the hand (i.e. unit of measure; here it would be a vine). — [b] i.e. worth. — [c] second 'thousand' is probably duplica- tion. — [d] i.e. of money. — [4] om. — [e] lit. fall. — [5] the mountains. — [f] lit. reach. — [6] om. — [7] the thorn. — [8] + and. — [9] om. — [10] for a new plant received the faith of God. — [11] and.

46.   † Isa 7:23-25.

never produced ᵍ fruit to God. ⌐He said, it says, 'as ¹² the plant';
faith ⌐should dwell ¹³ in us ⌐as a seed ¹⁴, that with joy we may produce ʰ
fruit to God.

47.   As Isaiah preached concerning the vineyard which was planted
5 and ⌐its fruit improved that it might be plucked up ¹, ⌐and spoke
concerning the desolate mountains, that it should become furrowed;
in like manner also it is written in Ezekiel that God had destroyed
the first plant as newly planted ᵃ men, and he caused other men to
rejoice, who were desolate and dried up in idolatry, and makes them
10 into glorious, beautiful trees, as from the first people, he takes the
plant, (and) engrafts into them Jesus Christ, that he might be taken
from the people of the House of Judah, after scorning the first kingdom; for more than all the sons of Israel which were called the scorned
and despised plant, the people of the House of Judah were great and
15 honorable, for Jesus Christ came forth from it.   Ezekiel the Prophet
† says, 'Thus says the Lord Almighty, I will take from the choice of
the top of the cedars and the cypress, and I will remove from the
highest, the shoot which (is) from the young shoots, and I will plant
them on a high mountain, and I will hang it from the high mountain
20 of Israel, I will plant and establish (it); it shall put forth branches
and shall bear fruit; and it shall become a great tree, and in the strength
of its branches the birds of the air shall rest, and all its branches in it
shall be restored ᵇ, and all the trees of the forest shall indeed know
that I am the Lord, that I bring down the high trees and raise up
25 the low trees, I dry up the green tree and I make green the dried
tree'.   Therefore in the parables our Lord likened us to plants of
trees and to the vine. ²

48.   ⌐And in this manner we are likened to plants; for at first a
shoot from the vines is planted simply alone (and) unadorned ᵃ in the
30 ground, and then it grows stronger, and it secretly receives strength
for the vine, and branches and leaves and blossoms and grapes, then
it becomes wine; and when a cutting from the vine is unadorned,

---

ᵍ lit. gave. — ¹² Moreover then as the seed and. — ¹³ dwelt. — ¹⁴ om. — ʰ lit. give.
    47.   ¹ was watered and it did not give fruit. — ᵃ see Arm text. — ᵇ lit. confirmed. —
² om.
    48.   ᵃ lit. bare.

    47.   † Ezk 17:22-24.

the laborer [b] is set [c] over it, who having cultivated around its roots, and having indeed cleaned its branches of dried ends and pulled the weeds and done all his work at the proper time, and with the watchful care of the laborer the vine receives the service [1] ⌜which is sent to it by God : sun, rain, clouds, dew [2] and gentle breezes, ⌜and it has [3] 5 good fruit, which makes [4] the lord of the vineyard joyful. But if [5] the laborer [6] despised it, and ⌜the nourishing nurse [d] is wanting in service to it [7], the vine ⌜indeed dries up [8] ⌜and the fruit which was prepared to be produced from it, is left destitute [e,9], and it ⌜becomes fuel [10] for tinder. In like manner also men who become disciples 10 in the Kingdom of Heaven and [11] monks are planted by faith; ⌜in this way [12] we rejoice [f,13] ⌜to call upon [14] the name of God ⌜and to believe [15] that there is only one God [16]; ⌜and at first we are without fruit, for in all labors and works we are novices [g], and then the teachers, in the likeness of the laborers, become our overseers [17].   15

49. And as the laborer [1] ⌜does all the work at the proper time [2] ⌜and cleans and prunes the vine [3], in like manner also ⌜the teachers present to us the instruction of the teaching, with wisdom and [4] encouragement, at the proper time, and [5] they rebuke us and ⌜show (us) [6] fear, ⌜and clean (and) take away from us all works of evil, as 20 thorns and thistles which the laborer gathers (and) takes away from the vineyard [7], and we receive [8] in the likeness of the rain [9], dew, ⌜sun, clouds, mist [10] and ⌜breezes [11] : the reading of the Scriptures, the interpretation, the prayers, and [12] consecration [a], and [13] the blessing of the praise of the sacrifice [b]; and ⌜with those we grow 25 and flourish [c] as a becoming vineyard, and we shall stand firm on the right hand of our Lord, when we shall have raised fruits of holiness pleasing to our Lord; and that they shall save us, our Lord witnessed

---

[b] i.e. field-laborer. — [c] lit. left. — [1] om. — [2] to God who sent to it rain, dew and clouds. — [3] that it shall have. —[4] made. — [5] because. — [6] laborers. — [d] i.e. over-seer. — [7] it lacked a nourisher and nurse .— [8] becomes dried up. — [e] or : becomes deprived. — [9] om. — [10] was fit. — [11] om. — [12] therefore. — [f] lit. refresh ourselves. [13] learn. — [14] om. — [15] om. — [16] and we believe in it. — [g] lit. children. — [17] om.

49. [1] + of the vineyard. — [2] om. — [3] takes care of, digs and prunes, and etc. — [4] we receive the instruction and admonition of the teachers who with. — [5] om. — [6] read : 'dissipate dread and' B. — [7] om. — [8] + from the teachers. — [9] om. — [10] and mist and sun. —[11] om. — [12] om. — [a] lit. laying on of hands. —[13] om. — [b] or : mass. — [c] or : rejoice. —

† concerning it and he says 14, 'Come blessed ones of my Father, ⌐in-
herit the Kingdom which shall have been prepared for you from the
foundation ᵈ of the world 15; for ⌐I was 16 hungered and you gave to
me to eat, ⌐I was thirsty and you gave to me to drink, I was a stranger
5 and you gathered ᵉ me, I was naked and you clothed me, I was sick
and you visited me, I was in prison and you came to me 17'.   And
⌐in this manner 18 we are like a plant.

50.   ⌐Now in what manner we are able to give pleasing ᵃ fruit
to God, or how we are able to give to eat to Christ, behold our Lord
† advises us when he says, he says, 'Truly I say to you 1, as much as 2
what you did to any 3 one of the least ᵇ of my brethren 4, you did
⊙ (it) to me'.   For ⌐Isaiah the Prophet foretold and he says, 'Behold
the virgin ᶜ shall conceive and bring forth a little child ᵈ and they
shall call his name Emmanuel, which interpreted is called, our God
15 with us'.   And in this manner Jesus became our God (who is) with us.
For he said, he says, 'whoever you honored, I shall be honored with
them', for he is with us and in us 5.   Now they who look down upon ᵉ
their 6 brethren 7, our Lord calls before the seat of judgment and he
is their accuser, ⌐as if they looked down upon ᶠ him 8.
20   51.   Moreover ⌐these in which faith was planted and they received ᵃ
not the service of the nourishment, those which we considered above,
they indeed dry up like a dried-up vine, and the beautiful fruit which
was prepared in them to come forth ᵇ, is indeed deprived.   And when
the Lord of the vineyard shall come to receive the fruitful fruit of
25 the vineyard, and he finds them desolate of good works, they are
rooted out and fall into tinder as the dried-up vine 1.   ⌐And as the
vine when it is planted, they do not go to dig (and) see if it might have

---

14 we produce the fruit which the Lord spoke of. — ᵈ lit. beginning. — 15 om. — 16 om. —
ᵉ or : received, welcomed. — 17 and etc. — 18 with all this fruitfulness.

50.   ᵃ or : acceptable. — 1 om. — 2 for with. — 3 om. — ᵇ lit. tiny. — 4 om. — ᶜ or :
maiden. — ᵈ or : boy. — 5 God became he who (is) Emmanuel, God with us ; and to anyone whom also we shall do, we do it to Christ ; for he is with us always. — ᵉ lit. cast down
their eyes from. — 6 him. — 7 om. — ᶠ lit. cast down their eyes from. — 8 om.

51.   ᵃ or : embraced. — ᵇ lit. become. — 1 those planted in the faith who do not
bring forth the fruits, which we considered above, as the dried-up vines shall be burned
in fire.

49.   † Mt 25:34b-36.
50.   † Mt 25:40bc. — ⊙ Mt 1:23.

taken hold and held fast on to fruit, but in a year it shows evidence
of leaves on its ends, and then afterwards it gives fruit. In like
manner also, when faith is planted in us and we have taken hold of (it),
someone does not come to our minds to enter (and) see if it might
have taken hold of (faith), or not [2]. But [3] as the vine ⌐that in a year 5
shows color when the leaves flourish, in like manner also, when faith
becomes confirmed in our minds, at first we bud, for he produces
love in our minds and it appears outwardly, and then we become
visibly fruitful [4]. ⌐And in this way our faith is likened to plants [5].

52. And [1] moreover our Lord likened his [2] Church to sheep [a,3], 10
⌐and he himself became the shepherd; as also in the Gospels there it
says [4], ⌐'Who shall there be of you who shall have sheep, and one †
sheep shall be lost [b]; will he not leave the ninety and nine on the
hill [c] in the wilderness [5] and ⌐go after the lost one (and) will search
until he will find it?'. And therefore he said to his disciples [6], 'Fear ☉
not little flock', and ⌐wherefore he says, 'Behold [7] I send you as ◓
lambs [8] ⌐among the wolves'. And with many parables he called the
disciples believers and sheep, and he himself became the shepherd [9].
Moreover in this manner the [10] Lord followed the Law and the Prophets,
for many prophets [11], kings and princes became [12] shepherds before 20
our Lord. Abel who was pleasing to God was at first a shepherd;
and Abraham, ⌐to whom [13] the testament of inheritance ⌐was put [14],
was a master of sheep; and God took Jacob from the shepherds and
spoke to him; and he took Moses from the sheep, and he became a
king and messenger [d] of God; and David was called from the sheep, 25
and he became king over Israel. And all these men became shepherds
of the pastures of men ⌐prior to [15] our Lord; because at first they
would learn from the sheep, what is the watchful care [e] of the shepherd
for his flocks, for when a lamb might go astray from the flock, he

---

[2] om. — [3] For. — [4] little by little puts forth leaves and then the fruit, in this same
manner at first we believe, and we bring forth love. — [5] om.

52. [1] om. — [2] the. — [a] or : 'flock of sheep'. — [3] a flock. — [4] om. — [b] or : stray. —
[c] or : mountain. — [5] he leaves, he says, the ninety and nine sheep. — [6] om. — [7] om. —
[8] sheep. — [9] om. — [10] our. — [11] righteous. — [12] were. — [13] who had. — [14] om. — [d] lit.
angel. — [15] according to the will of. — [e] or : guardianship.

52.   † Lk 15:4. — ☉ Lk 12:32. — ◓ Lk 10:3.

⌜will search for and bring and put ¹⁶ it in his arms, and he ⌜will join ᶠ,¹⁷
it to its companions; and ¹⁸ he knows how necessary it is to feed the
sick, and to anoint the leprous, and to bind ᵍ the broken.

53. ⌜Since they will know how ¹ the shepherd humbles himself
⁵ ⌜and toils for his flock, in like manner, he will be careful with the
pasture of men. And Ezekiel the Prophet also bears witness con-
† cerning these ², 'The Word ᵃ of the Lord was upon me, and he says,
'Son of man prophesy against ᵇ the shepherds ³ of Israel and you shall
say to them ⁴, thus says the Lord Almighty; O shepherds of Israel,
¹⁰ can it be that shepherds would feed themselves? ⌜Do not shepherds
feed the sheep ⁵? Now behold, you consume ᶜ the milk ⁶, you clothe
yourselves delicately ⁷, you eat the fats ⁸, and you feed not my sheep;
you healed ⁹ not the sick, and you strengthened ¹⁰ not the weak,
you bound ¹¹ not the broken, and ¹² you comforted ¹³ not the suffering,
¹⁵ you did ¹⁴ not bring back those gone astray and ¹⁵ you did ¹⁶ not
search for the lost; you overthrew ᵈ,¹⁷ the very strong maliciously ᵉ,
you tormented ¹⁸ the powerful ᶠ with violence and with fraud; and
my sheep were scattered, because there was ¹⁹ not a shepherd for
them; and they became meat ᵍ for the wild beasts ʰ of the wilderness;
²⁰ ⌜my sheep were scattered (and) gone astray to all the high mountains ²⁰, they were scattered throughout the earth, and there was no
one who ⌜searched for (them), nor those who ²¹ brought (them) back.
Therefore ⌜shepherds, hear you all the Word of the Lord. I am
alive ²² says the Lord Almighty, because ⌜my sheep became a prey,
²⁵ and my sheep were meat ⁱ for all the wild beasts ʲ of the wilderness ᵏ,
because there was not a shepherd over them and they did not go out
in search for my sheep, but they were feeding themselves and were
not feeding my sheep ²³, for this reason, ⌜shepherds, hear the Word

---

¹⁶ searches and puts. — ᶠ lit. mix it with. — ¹⁷ joins. — ¹⁸ om. — ᵍ lit. enclose.

53. ¹ how as. — ² to the flock, in like manner also he will be careful also with the
pastures of men; even Ezekiel the prophet writes. — ᵃ or : oracle. — ᵇ lit. over. —
³ sons. — ⁴ the shepherds of Israel. — ⁵ and would not feed the sheep? — ᶜ lit. eat. —
⁶ add : 'and' B. — ⁷ add : 'and' B. — ⁸ add : 'and clothe yourselves with wool' B. —
⁹ heal. — ¹⁰ strengthen. — ¹¹ bind. — ¹² om. — ¹³ comfort. — ¹⁴ do. — ¹⁵ om. — ¹⁶ do. —
ᵈ or : laid waste. — ¹⁷ overthrow. — ᵉ or : with fraud. — ¹⁸ overthrow (lit. kill). —
ᶠ or : valiant. — ¹⁹ is. — ᵍ or : food. — ʰ or : beasts. — ²⁰ om. — ²¹ om. — ²² thus. —
ⁱ or : food. — ʲ or : beasts. — ᵏ or : desert. — ²³ you acted in this manner and my sheep
were scattered.

53. † Ezk 34:1-13a.

of the Lord, thus says the Lord Almighty [24], behold I have come (and)
taken in hand [1] those shepherds and I will require my sheep at their [25]
hands, and [26] I shall stop the shepherds of my sheep and they shall
feed my sheep no more, and I shall save my sheep from their mouths,
and no more will they be meat for them. ⌜Thus says the Lord Al- 5
mighty : behold, I will examine my sheep, and I will make an inspection of my sheep, as the shepherd should make an inspection of
his flock on a dark and foggy day, thus I shall search for them and
shall gather them from all places, where (ever) they may be scattered
on the dark day (and) on the foggy day; and I will take them away 10
from the Gentiles [m], and I will gather them from the countries'. And
moreover he says, 'I myself will feed my sheep, and I will give repose ⊙
to them, says the Lord All-powerful, I will search for the lost, I will
bring back that which went astray, I will bind the broken, I will
strengthen the sick, I will guard [n] the fat and the strong [o] and I will 15
feed them with justice and with righteousness [p,27]'. In this manner
he made clear ⌜to us [28] that he [29] rejects [q] all kings and princes. ⌜More-
over the Lord Almighty says, 'Behold I have taken you in hand [r]; ●
I will judge [s] sheep with sheep, I will judge the strong [t] with the
weak [u], and the weak with the strong; because you strong indeed 20
struck and trampled upon the weak until you drove (them) out and
my sheep were scattered. Therefore I shall save my sheep, and no
more will I abandon them to prey [v,30]; and I will judge ram with ram,
and he-goat with he-goat [31]. And I will indeed set over them one
shepherd, my servant David, who [32] will tend [w] them, and he will 25
give them repose, and he shall be their shepherd'.

54. The words of the Prophets are always [1] true, but these two
words are varied to one another, because at first he says, 'I shall be
their shepherd', and afterwards he says, 'David my shepherd will

---

[24] thus says the Lord Almighty, shepherds, hear my words. — [1] lit. reached upon (or :
taken over). — [25] your. — [26] om. — [m] or : heathen. — [n] or : keep. — [o] or : valiant. —
[p] or : equity. — [27] And as the shepherd makes an inspection of his flocks, in the same
manner also I will do (that); and I will gather the scattered from all peoples and from
the Gentiles, and I will enclose the wounded and the suffering, and. — [28] om. — [29] the
Lord. — [q] lit. drives out. — [r] lit. reached upon (or : taken over you). — [s] or : discern. —
[t] or : rich. — [u] or : poor. — [v] or: permit them to prey. — [30] om. — [31] + my sheep. —
[32] read : 'and he' B. — [w] or : pasture; feed.

54. [1] om.

53. ⊙ Ezk 34:15-16. — ● Ezk 34:20b-23.

tend them'. Nevertheless these words are the same and ² equal to
one another, when one takes the shepherd to be one who is God and
man; that ³ our Lord himself is, ⌐for he ⁴ was born from the descendants of David and he is God, for both are accomplished in him.
₅ And Isaiah ⌐the Prophet ⁵ bears witness that by birth God is savior,
† he says, 'A child was born to us, and ⁶ a son was given to us; ⌐and his ⁷
government ᵃ shall be bestowed ᵇ on his shoulders; ⌐his name shall
be called, wonderful counselor, God, mighty'; for Christ was God,
and the Son of God ⁸. Therefore it was indeed fulfilled ⌐in him ⁹,
₁₀ that which God says, 'I shall be the shepherd of my sheep, and I will
feed them'. And because he is the son of David, (and) David himself
became a shepherd, he also fulfilled ¹⁰ the Word which God spoke
⌐to them ¹¹, 'David my shepherd shall pasture them, and he shall be
the shepherd over them'.
₁₅   55. And if anyone shall say to me that because he is the son of ·
David, how ⌐is it ¹ possible to call him David and for David to fulfill ²
the pastorship ᵃ, it is easy for me to show in Holy Scripture that he
is called David who (is) from the descendants of David and has the
throne of his kingdom. For it is written in the Books of Kings, at
₂₀ the time when the hosts of the sons of Israel came and they say to
† Rehoboam the son of Solomon, 'Relieve us ᵇ of the taxes ᶜ of your
⊙ father ³', he says to them, 'My little finger is larger ᵈ than the thumb
of my father; my father chastised you with a whip, but I will chas-
⊃ tise ᵉ (you) with iron rods'. And ⁴ they say ⌐to him, 'And ⁵ hence-
₂₅ forth we have no ᶠ portion in David, nor inheritance in the son of
Jesse. Now go everyone to your tents ᵍ, sons of Israel; now see
your own house, David'. Not that David was there, but his son.
For if this one who (is) only a descendant ⌐who is ⁶ born from the
house of David, and (who) according ʰ to the justice and the works
₃₀ and the power ⁱ of David was small, and (who) reigned over only

---

² (and). — ³ om. — ⁴ he who. — ⁵ om. — ⁶ del : om B. — ⁷ the. — ᵃ or : rule. — ᵇ lit.
given (or : put). — ⁸ om. — ⁹ om. — ¹⁰ + in him. — ¹¹ he says.

    55. ¹ shall it be. — ² + in him. — ᵃ or : leadership. — ᵇ lit. lighten from us. —
ᶜ or : services. — ³ + and. — ᵈ or : thicker. — ᵉ or : discipline. — ⁴ om. — ⁵ om. —
ᶠ lit. there is not for us a. — ᵍ or : dwellings. — ⁶ (and) was. — ʰ lit. from. — ⁱ or : rule. —

---

    54. † Isa 9:6.
    55. † I Kg 12:4b (Paraphrase). — ⊙ I Kg 12:10b,11b. — ⊃ I Kg 12:16b.

the two nations, (if) he was called David, how much more Christ
(should be called David)? For he was born from the people of the
house of David, and [j] his [7] works and justice [8] and ⌐power [k] are [9]
very great (and) [10] excellent, ⌐and he caused his name to shine from
one end of the heavens to the other end of that same [11]; and [12] his [5]
teaching [13] was proclaimed, and his kingdom was established in every
place [14]. Therefore ⌐it is right to call him [15] David, ⌐and he fulfilled [16]
through him the pastorship of David. And as David was at first a
shepherd and then became king, after the same manner also, ⌐at
first [17] Christ previously was for us a shepherd, and those gone astray [10]
he turned back to life, and healed the sick and [18] strengthened the
weak and cleansed the leprous; and then afterwards ⌐he became [19]
king, and [20] he comes at his second coming (as) the mighty [21] king,
and the glorious God. And in this way the Church (is) [22] likened to
sheep and Christ to the shepherd.   [15]

56. ⌐And in order that he might make clear that men are called
the sheep of the pasture, Ezekiel spoke in this manner from the same
oracle, 'But you my sheep, the sheep of my pasture, are men and I †
am your God, says the Lord Almighty'. Therefore even Christ, in
order that he might make clear that (men) are entirely [1] the same [20]
as in the above prophecy, ⌐he also called men who hearkened to him
sheep, and he became a shepherd for them [2]. ⌐Therefore our Lord [3]
said, 'I came not to dissolve [a] the Law or the Prophets, ⌐I came not ⊙
to dissolve [4] but to fulfill'. And after comparison [b,5] we agree [6]
that all these shepherds, whose names I considered, are likened to [25]
Christ; they killed some of them, and some of them escaped from
death and became [7] kings [8]; all these men are [9] in the likeness ⌐of
the image [10] of the forms of Christ. And as the image [c] of the king is
painted [d] in his childhood and ⌐in his [11] youth and old age and during
(his) reign, in like manner also all these shepherds in their times (were) [12] [30]

---

[j] lit. for. — [7] the. — [8] powers he did. — [k] lit. rights. — [9] justice was. — [10] and. — [11] om.
— [12] for. — [13] kingdom. — [14] land. — [15] he was called. — [16] in order to fulfill. — [17] came.
— [18] om. — [19] (as). — [20] om. — [21] great. — [22] is.

56. [1] For Christ is. — [2] om. — [3] as he also. — [a] or : loose. — [4] om. — [b] lit. when
having compared. — [5] + with the Scriptures. — [6] + (and) we find. — [7] were. — [8] + and.
— [9] were. — [10] om. — [c] lit. images. — [d] or : described. — [11] om. — [12] were.

56. † Ezk 34:31. — ⊙ Mt 5:17.

in the image of the forms of Christ; for the image of the king which
they paint in his childhood is not large [e], but it keeps the likeness
of (his) childhood; and moreover ⌜they set [13] up another image of
him when he becomes a man; likewise also, this image [14] keeps the
5 likeness of (his) time; and when he becomes king, moreover they
paint another one of him.   In like manner also (are) these which I
considered, because they kept the likeness of the forms of Christ;
⌜and they were painted of him, each of them with the likeness of one
or the other of the times of Christ [15], in which also [16] they were repre-
10 sented by him and they kept (it).

57.   Abel became a shepherd, a priest and was wounded; and he
took of his first-born [a] sheep, and he offered a sacrifice to God and
the sacrifice which he offered of his sheep on the altar with the in-
tention [b] of satisfaction was acceptable; and [1] after this the elder
15 brother ⌜of the same [2] killed him, and [3] he deceived [c] him.   And
because the Most High knew the deception [d] in the heart of Cain,
he did not receive his sacrifice.   In like manner also Christ became
a shepherd, a priest and was wounded, because [4] he offered a sacrifice
to God, and then [5] he was wounded at the hands of people who were
20 older than him by birth, for they betrayed [e] him and delivered [f] him
up.   And as God [6] did not receive the sacrifices [7] of Cain because
he doubted [g], and his hands were stained with blood because he was
(so) full of anger he killed his brother, and the killed sacrifice became
acceptable, in like manner also God receives our sacrifices, because
25 we follow the shepherd, the priest and the one who was killed : and [8]
the Israelites, who do not acknowledge Christ, because he would
sacrifice it [9] to God his Father, and [10] (who) stood in the will of Herod
and (who) follow the murderous Pharisees, nor are they acceptable
at the altar for satisfaction, because they partake of and are parties
30 to the blood of Christ.

†   58.   Isaiah the Prophet says 'I have had my fill [a], now it is enough
for me, burnt-offerings of rams and fat of lambs and blood of your

---

[e] or : great. — [13] he sets. — [14] + also. — [15] om. — [16] om.

57.   [a] or : eldest. — [b] or : desire for. — [1] om. — [2] his. — [3] read : 'for' B. — [c] or :
betrayed. — [d] or : betrayal. — [4] and. — [5] om. — [e] or : deceived. — [f] or : betrayed. —
[6] he. — [7] sacrifice. — [g] lit. his mind was divided. — [8] but. — [9] them. — [10] om.

58.   [a] or : I am full.

58.   † Isa 1:11b-15.

bulls and he-goats ⌐I do not want to see [1], and none of your appearance [b] do I want [2]. ⌐Who required this of your hands; then all of
you do not continue to trample my courts. If you shall offer to me
the fine flour [c] for sacrifice, it is in vain [d] for you; and if you cast
incense to me, that also is considered an abomination to me. Your [5]
new moons and your sabbaths I disapprove; your important days
I do not accept; your fasts and idleness and chief anniversaries [e] my
soul hated, and I have had my fill of you [f]. It is impossible, hereafter
I will forgive your sins no more; when you shall stretch forth your
hands to me, I will turn my face [g] from you. And if you shall continue [10]
to offer your prayers, I will not listen [h] to you, for your hands are full
of blood [3]⌐. And [4] the Prophet made clear and showed to us that
prayer and truth [i] are the end of immolations and sacrifices; and
they who participate in killing and are stained with blood, ⌐not even [5]
their prayers are [6] acceptable, because ⌐they are in fact sacrifices [7] [15]
as Cain's sacrifices ⌐which were not acceptable [8]. And [9] we who
follow Christ, who is likened to Abel in [j] his righteousness and priesthood and death, our sacrifices shall be accepted [10] on the altar; for
by the Father of the true [11], just shepherd we are offered without
sin on the altar; as also the Apostle says, 'I pray you, brethren, pre- ⊙
pare your members [k,12] (as) a living sacrifice, holy (and) pleasing [l] to
God'. And moreover ⌐he says [13], 'Daily [m] we are [14] counted [15] as ◖
sheep for the slaughter'. And in this way we are like [16] sheep. And
see, that ⌐Abel was likened [17] ⌐to the shepherd, to the [18] righteousness
⌐of Christ [19] and ⌐to his [20] priesthood and death.   [25]

    59. Jacob the Patriarch ⌐of the Fathers [1], was a shepherd of
Isaac his Father, and he was persecuted by his brothers who were
older than he, and then he [2] received his Syrian sheep. In like manner
also Christ became a teacher [3] to the Jews, to the first sheep; and

---

[1] om. — [b] or : presentation. — [2] + to see. — [c] lit. finest quality of wheat flour. —
[d] or : useless. — [e] or: feasts. — [f] or : I am satiated by you. — [g] or : eyes. — [h] or : hear.
— [3] om. — [4] Behold. — [i] lit. verity. — [5] om. — [6] + not. — [7] their sacrifice is not
acceptable. — [8] om. — [9] But. — [j] lit. with. — [10] acceptable. — [11] innocent. — [k] or :
whole bodies. — [12] read : 'bodies' B. — [l] or: acceptable. — [13] om. — [m] or: the whole day.
— [14] om. — [15] + ourselves. — [16] counted (as). — [17] he was like the first Abel in. —
[18] om. — [19] om. — [20] om.
    59. [1] om. — [2] add : 'he came (and)' B. — [3] read : 'shepherd' B.

58. ⊙ Rom 12:1. — ◖ Rom 8:36b.

when he was persecuted by ⌐Herod the king [4], he became a shepherd [5]
of the Syrian heathens [a]. ⌐In the time when Jacob became shepherd
of the sheep of Laban, Laban divided his own sheep with Jacob,
so that every lamb which shall be dappled and speckled, that one
5 shall be for Jacob, and the sheep entirely of one color, that one shall
be for Laban. Jacob painted the rods according to the Word of the
Lord, and cast (them) before the sheep, and the offspring of the sheep
were like the color of the appearance of the painted rods [6]. And
⌐the sheep followed the just shepherd to the holy [b] land of the Is-
10 raelites, which they had not seen. The mothers of one common color
who gave birth to the varigated lambs, were reared in the impure
land [7]; in like manner also we were delivered [c] from heathenism, and
are spotted (and) speckled with the white marks in the likeness of the
cross according to the marks of the rods; and we are not like [8] our
15 ungodly [9] fathers from which we are begotten [d]; and according to
the likeness of the sheep of Jacob we follow the just shepherd to the
holy land, and [10] to the inheritance of Israel. And our [11] fathers
which begot [e] us in heathenism, and the marks on the rods do not
appear on them, they remain in the impure land. And as Jacob at
20 his persecution turned foreign sheep to the land of Israel, in like
manner also Christ when he was persecuted by the Jews, he turned
heathen men [12] to the worship of his God, and to the first inheritance
of Israel. And as the sheep of Jacob ⌐are nothing like [13] those sheep
which begot them, in like manner also we are nothing [14] like our
25 heathen fathers; for we were indeed attracted by [f] the rods, and we
became like them [g,15]. And in this way ⌐we are likened to sheep, and
Christ to the shepherd [16]. ⌐These are the marks of Christ which
were represented [h] by Jacob in his pastorship and persecution, because
he turned foreign sheep to the land of Israel with the marks on the
30 rods [17].

    60. Concerning Joseph, whose elder brothers were also [1] shep-

---

[4] the Jews. — [5] teacher. — [a] or : Gentiles. — [6] om. — [b] or : blessed. — [7] the flock
which gave birth to the varigated lambs for Jacob which went to the holy land of the Jews,
they themselves remained in the impure land for Laban. — [c] lit. born. — [8] imitators
of. — [9] read : 'heathen' B. — [d] lit. born. — [10] om. — [11] the. — [e] lit. gave birth to. —
[12] om. — [13] were not like. — [14] not. — [f] lit. indeed carried away in us the love of. —
[g] lit. became imitators of them. — [15] the sheep. — [16] Christ pastures (them). — [h] or :
described (lit. painted). — [17] om.

    60. [1] om.

herds : ⸢his father sent him to go (and) to see his shepherd brothers,
and the shepherd brothers had great envy towards him because the
father was fond of [a] him, and they considered (how) to kill him.   And
according to the word of Judah, Joseph was sold for the price of
silver, and they sent his garment to the father, as if he shall have   5
been torn by a wild beast.   And when this persecuted, wounded
and sold one went into the land where they knew him not, he became
the feeder-savior of all the inhabitants of the land.   Because the
king of Egypt had made him lord over the nourishment of the living,
and food was not found elsewhere, whoever went up and subjected   10
themselves under the hand of Joseph, lived.   Likewise when his
brothers came and prostrated themselves to him [2], he fed them with
food [b].   In like manner also ⸢Christ, his brothers [3] were older shepherds [4]; God his [5] Father sent him to see the shepherds [6] and their
sheep [7], and his brothers the Israelites considered (how to bring)   15
death upon him, because they had envy toward him; and according
to the word of Judah he was sold and was killed; not only that, he
died after being wounded; and after he was sold, ⸢the Eternal King
made him lord over the nourishment of the living [8], and everyone
whoever is confirmed in him, he feeds with food.   And as the brothers   20
of Joseph when they prostrated themselves to him they were fed
more than ⸢every man [9], in like manner also (are) the Israelites, for
they are ⸢in fact [10] the killers, the sellers [11] and the persecutors [12];
when they come and subject themselves to Christ, they find life from
him, and they become respectable.   And as in that time there was   25
great famine in every land and all men individually went [c,13] to buy
their food in order to live; and ⸢when the sons of Israel went and
brought their food from Joseph, they strengthened their hearts with
food, but they were not indeed satisfied until they went into the city,
in which the wounded and sold one had become a lord; and to him   30
was gathered and prepared the storehouses of life [14].   In like manner

---

[a] lit. loved. — [2] He was sent to his brothers who were envious (of him); according
to the mouth of Judah, they sold (him), and this wounded one became a ruler
of Egypt, and lord and feeder of all peoples; and when his brothers came to him. —
[b] lit. bread. — [3] the brothers of Christ. — [4] and the shepherds of Israel. — [5] the. —
[6] sheep. — [7] shepherds. — [8] however, he became lord over all the living and ruler for
his Eternal Father always. — [9] other men. — [10] om. — [11] persecutors. — [12] sellers. —
[c] lit. go. — [13] read : 'were going' B. — [14] the sons of Israel who were not satisfied with
the food which they brought until they went to the wounded Joseph in Egypt.

also in present times there is great famine, for we all ⌜shall be ¹⁵ hungry
for ᵈ the Word of God and we all have the instruction of the teaching,
and we strengthened our hearts only with the Word of ⌜our Lord ¹⁶,
and as much as we feed (on) him, the more we want ⌜of ᵉ him; and
₅ when we ¹⁷ go to Christ, for he himself is wounded and sold, and we
dwell in the country ᶠ of life, in which Christ ⌜is lord ᵍ, then in that
time we are indeed satisfied ¹⁸. And as ⌜the sons of Jacob went to
buy their food and indeed received food and did not give their silver
in its respective weight, in like manner also we indeed receive life
₁₀ free (of cost) and give nothing, yet we receive life without silver, as
also the Prophet said. As the brothers did not recognize Joseph
at the time because he became a minister ʰ for the king and was the
lord and prince over life, because he became great (and) surpassed
very much from that time since they killed and sold him ¹⁹, ⌜since they
₁₅ did not believe ²⁰ that he could ²¹ be alive, in like manner also ²²
Christ, when his killers, persecutors and sellers see him ²³, ⌜they do
not recognize him on account of his greatness, since ²⁴, because of
that, they do ²⁵ not believe that he could really ¹ be alive. And in
all this Christ is likened ²⁶ to a commander of sheep. And Joseph
₂₀ tended and kept the form of the pastorship of Christ even by his ²⁷
death and being sold and ²⁸ feeding.

61. Moreover David was a shepherd and the younger ⌜of his brothers ¹, and God was pleased with him when Saul the king ⌜at first
did not know ² him; but Saul called him, and he approached by himself
₂₅ in order that he might kill Goliath the giant, because he was battling
with ᵃ the sons of Israel ⌜and they were not able to oppose him ³.
But when David ⌜saw Goliath and killed him ⁴, the daughters of
Israel ⁵ blessed David ⁶ and praised him, and Saul had envy toward
David (and) persecuted him. In like manner also Christ first became

---

¹⁵ are. — ᵈ lit. with. — ¹⁶ of God, as (was) brought with bread to Jacob. — ᵉ lit. with. — ¹⁷
to. — ᶠ or : region. — ᵍ or : reigns. — ¹⁸ dwells, and in that time then we are filled with
satisfaction. — ʰ or : steward. — ¹⁹ the brothers received wheat free (of cost), and they
brought the silver to the same one; in like manner also we received life without payment
and price, as the Prophet says; and since that day they sold Joseph, he became very
great; and his brothers, the killers, did not recognize him. — ²⁰ om. — ²¹ add : 'really' B.
— ²² om. — ²³ om. — ²⁴ they are astonished. — ²⁵ did. — ¹ lit. absolutely. — ²⁶ like.
— ²⁷ om. — ²⁸ but also his.

61. ¹ om. — ² was before. — ᵃ or : making war on. — ³ om. — ⁴ killed Goliath. —
⁵ Jerusalem. — ⁶ om.

a shepherd, for he was in fact a teacher. When the sons of Israel
were oppressed by evil spirits and by defeats [b], and when he healed
them ⌐of insufferable [c] defeats, and [7] his power appeared ⌐to the
people and [8] they praised him, Herod had envy ⌐towards him (and) [9]
persecuted him. When Saul sent (someone) in order to kill [10] David, [5]
he escaped ⌐from the killer [11] from [d] the wicked king, who was [12]
signified [13] to be king for [14] a little while, and he became a righteous
king. In like manner also Christ escaped from death, ⌐from the
killer [15] from Herod the wicked king, and he became an Eternal King
after escaping from death. Abel the shepherd first depicted [e] the [10]
killing of Christ, for truly he was killed; and David another shepherd
depicted the resurrection of ⌐Christ from [16] the dead, for he truly
escaped from the killing, and became king. And in this manner
the Church of our Lord is likened to sheep, and he ⌐is likened [17] to a
shepherd.   [15]

   62.   And as the shepherd, that goes at the head of the sheep into
every place; into the rough [a] and soft (places) and into the mountains
and the valleys, into the dry (places) and into the marshes, and the
sheep follow him; in like manner also Christ, everything whatever
he taught us, he first did that, and ⌐through that (means) [1] he went [20]
before us, so that we [2] might follow him. For he taught us, ⌐he says [3],
'Happy [b] ⌐shall it be [4] for the poor ⌐in [c] spirit [5]'; he in fact became †
poor before us, as also [6] the Apostle [7] says ⌐in the second letter to
the Corinthians, he says [8], 'You know not [d] the grace of our Lord ⊙
⌐Jesus Christ [9], that for your sakes ⌐the rich [10] ⌐from his riches [11] [25]
became poor, that you through his poverty might become rich',
And our Lord taught us that he was reviled [12] and was killed for our
sakes, since [13] he said ⌐to us, he says [14], 'Happy ⌐shall it be [15] for you ◖
when they shall ⌐revile you [16], and shall say an evil thing about you';
as in the first place his name was reviled, when he was kind to every [30]

---

[b] lit. bruises. — [c] lit. very bad. — [7] om. — [8] (and). — [9] and. — [10] persecute. — [11] om. —
[d] lit. of. — [12] om. — [13] + him. — [14] in. — [15] om. — [e] lit. painted. — [16] om. — [17] om.

   62.   [a] or : difficult. — [1] om. — [2] + also. — [3] om. — [b] or : blessed. — [4] om. — [c] lit.
with. — [5] and. — [6] om. — [7] + he. — [8] dcl : om B. — [d] insertion of 'not' is probably
copyist error. — [9] om. — [10] read : 'he who was rich' B. — [11] om. — [12] persecuted. —
[13] and. — [14] om. — [15] is it. — [16] persecute you and revile (you).

   62.   † Mt 5:3a. — ⊙ II Cor 8:9. — ◖ Mt 5:11.

man who approached him. Since he taught us that when we die, we live, he died before us, and he arose from the dead. Since he promised to seat us [17] at the right hand of God [18] his Father, he ascended before us to the celestial kingdom [19], and entirely (by) himself,

5 beforehand, he paved [e] the way for us [20], as the shepherd that [21] goes before his sheep.

63. ⌐But nevertheless we should know [1] this, that all sheep follow the [2] paths ⌐of the shepherd [3] everywhere, and ⌐the lamb which goes [4] astray from the sheep and [5] from the paths of the shepherd, also [6]

10 becomes carrion and meat [a] for the ravenous wolves and for the greedily hungered [7] wild beasts. In like manner also we; every church which is itself the sheep, follows the path [8]; and ⌐the person [9] who separates himself from the flock of the sheep, which is itself the Church, and ⌐he goes astray [10] from the path of the Shepherd Christ, he goes to

15 perdition [11], extermination and torments of fire. And every church follows the just shepherd [12], and is gathered together to him, in the region [b] of life. And in this way we are likened to sheep.

64. And [1] more than all this [2], our Lord likened those who are carried away by the invitation and our [3] affection and the ravish-

20 ment, and [4] our minds ⌐are strewn with it [5] and we are tied to it - - he likened [6] us to the ⌐habitation [a] of the [7] world here, to the bride and bridegroom, for those strangers who profaned them, and say that they are impure [b]; and our Lord compared his path [8] to this symbol,

† for John says, 'He who has the bride [c], he is the bridegroom'. Al-

25 though [9] this is not written for the strangers (in their Gospels), nevertheless to them there, that which is written in the Gospels (is) indeed also [10] for them, and as us they read, ⌐it says [11], thus our Lord says,

⊙ ⌐'you cannot [d,12] order the bridegroom's companions to fast, as long as the bridegroom shall be with them'. And he made clear and showed

---

[17] (us). — [18] om. — [19] dwelling. — [e] or : cleared. — [20] + now. — [21] he.

63. [1] And he knows. — [2] his. — [3] om. — [4] if any indeed go. — [5] om. — [6] om. — [a] or : food. — [7] which tear to pieces. — [8] + of the Shepherd Christ. — [9] that one. — [10] om. — [11] + and. — [12] add : 'Christ' B. — [b] or : country.

64. [1] om. — [2] read : 'others' B. — [3] his. — [4] om. — [5] it received. — [6] compared. — [a] or : custom. — [7] physical. — [b] or : unclean. — [8] paths. — [c] lit. to whom there is a bride. — [9] Since. — [10] om. — [11] for. — [d] lit. it is not possible for you to. — [12] It is not for you to.

64. † Jn 3:29a. — ⊙ Lk 5:34. —

us that he himself is the bridegroom and we are his table companions
and his friends of the bridegroom.   Moreover the Apostle says in the
Letter to the Ephesians, ⌐thus he says[13], 'Each man[14] should love his ◖
wife as himself, as also Christ loved[15] his Church, ⌐because we are members of his body[16]'; in like manner also you[17], each one[18] of you individ-   5
ually ought to love his wife as himself, as also Christ loved his[19]
Church[20].   'Therefore a man shall leave his father and mother, and ⌖
shall follow[e] his wife, and the two shall be one flesh.   This is a great
mystery, but I speak in Christ and in the Church'.

65.   Moreover in this manner our Book fulfilled the chief prophecy, 10
which is written by Isaiah the Prophet, ⌐he says[1], 'As the bridegroom †
rejoices over[a] the bride, in the same manner your God rejoices[2] over
you; and as a young man ⌐shall settle[3] with the virgin[b], in this same
manner shall your sons settle in you'.   And moreover David says,
'Their voice went out to all the earth, and[4] their words[5] to the ends ◉
of the world; he pitched his tent in the sun, and he ⌐comes forth like
the bridegroom[6] from his chamber'.   And the prophets always speak
concerning the people[7] of the Church : when it causes[c] itself[8] to fear
God, and cares[d] for him as for a bridegroom and ⌐(as) the care of the
wife for her husband[e]; and[9] they read these parts even with distrust; 20
and[10] having doubted, the people are divided as a women who ⌐is
separated from and distrusts[11] her husband, and she commits adultery
with someone.

66.   Jeremiah the Prophet says concerning the first people.   'Be- †
hold I judge you[1], because you say[2]', ⌐he says[3], 'I have not sinned[4], 25
now that you have become mad (enough) to relate your ways, even
by the Egyptians you shall be put to shame, according to the shame
which you were put by the Assyrians.   Even from that[5] also you

---

[13] om. — [14] om. — [15] om. — [16] om. — [17] om. — [18] om. — [19] om. — [20] + for we are
members of his body. — [e] or : go after.

65.   [1] om. — [a] or : is delighted with. — [2] shall rejoice. — [3] settles. — [b] or : maiden. —
[4] om. — [5] + are. — [6] (is) as a bridegroom that comes forth. — [7] Jews. — [c] lit. gives. —
[8] also. — [d] or : serves. — [e] text is corrupt here, see Codex B. — [9] read : 'she marries him,
as also the woman her man; since they do not attend to this' B. — [10] for. — [11] read :
'having doubted, is separated from' B.

66.   [1] + and. — [2] were saying. — [3] om. — [4] + at all. — [5] this.

64.   ◖ Eph 5:28a,29b-30. ⌖ Eph 5:31,32.
65.   † Isa 62:5b,5a. — ◉ Ps 19:4,5a.
66.   † Jer 2:35b-3:3.

shall go forth with (your) hands on (your) head, for the Lord was angry on account of the shoulders of your refuge, and you shall not prosper with them [6]; they say, If a man shall give up his wife, and ⌐the wife [7] shall go ⌐from him [8]; and [9] she shall become another man's, and if he shall indeed [10] return again to her [11], behold that woman would indeed be impure; and you committed adultery (and) were prostituted with many shepherds. Return to me, says the Lord Almighty [12]; lift up your eyes to the roads, and see, what place ⌐is there [13] which shall not be polluted [a] by you? You prepared yourself for them on the roads as a crow in the wilderness; you polluted [b] the land with your prostitution ⌐and with your wickedness [14]; and the rain was withheld ⌐in the heavens [15], and the dew did not bedew; and a shameless and [16] indecent face you made for yourself as a prostitute'. And moreover he says, 'As the wife (who) cheats her companion, in like manner the sons of Israel cheated [c] me [17]'.

† 67. Moreover Ezekiel ⌐the Prophet [1] says, 'The Word of the Lord was ⌐upon me [2] and he says, 'Son of Man go (and) rebuke Jerusalem and ⌐cause her to remember [a,3] her abomination [b]; and you shall say ⌐to her [4], thus says the Lord Almighty to Jerusalem : Was not your tribe [c,5] Canaanite; ⌐your father was an Amorite [8] and your mother a Hittite; ⌐(concerning) your birth, on the day that they gave birth to you [7], no one has [8] cut off your navel, and no one had washed you with water for salvation [9], ⌐and no (one) had salted you with salt, and [10] no (one) had wrapped you in swaddling clothes; because my eyes did not spare you, nor did I for you ⌐any one of [11] all these things ⌐or take care (of you), that some lamentation might pass [12] to you; but having been cast (out), you laid [13] on the face of the field because of your perverse mind and your hardened [14] heart. ⌐On the day in which they gave birth to you [15], I passed by you and saw you drenched with blood, and ⌐I said to you, be lifted up from

---

[6] + and. — [7] read : 'she' B. — [8] om. — [9] (and). — [10] om. — [11] her man. — [12] + and. — [13] shall there be. — [a] lit. soiled. — [b] lit. soiled. — [14] om. — [15] del : om B. — [16] om. — [c] or : belied. — [17] om.

67. [1] om. — [2] om. — [a] or : remind her of. — [3] tell her. — [b] or : impurity. — [4] om. — [c] or : generation. — [5] father. — [6] om. — [7] om. — [8] read : 'had' B. — [9] read : 'cleanliness' B. — [10] om. — [11] om. — [12] which happened. — [13] were. — [14] hard. — [15] and.

66. ⊙ Jer 3:20.
67. † Ezk 16:1-24.

your blood, and your life shall be raised up from the blood, be indeed
increased with cleanliness. I made you as a green [d] plant in the
field; and you increased and grew, and you came and entered into
the great cities [e,16]. Your breasts were formed [f] and (your) hair
(had) come forth [g], ⌐and you were naked [h] and bare [i]; I passed by 5
you [j] and saw that you were no longer a child [k] and the time for your
veils (had come); I spread my wings over you and I covered your
nakedness, and I swore to you and entered into a firm covenant with
you, says the Lord Almighty. And I brought you (as) the bride for
me, and I washed you with water and cleaned your blood [l] from you, 10
and I cleaned and anointed you with oil; I adorned you with various
attire [m] : I clothed you in purple and red, I adorned you and I brought
to your bosom fine linen, and I spread silk about you; and I adorned
you with ornaments [17] : I put [18] bracelets on your arms, and ⌐I put
a necklace on your neck, I put ear-rings on your ears, and I put ear 15
drops [n] with your ears, and I put [19] a crown ⌐of glory [20] on your head;
⌐I adorned you always with gold (and) silver [21], and I made your
garments [22] (with) fine linen and your finery (with) silk, satin [23], and
embroidery. I clothed you ⌐and made [o] your food with fine flour
and honey and olive oil; you ate and became soft and abounded; 20
you became beautiful and you fondled with the delicacies of royalty [p];
and the reputation [q] of your beauty went to all the nations [r], for I put
the grace of beauty upon your loveliness, says the Lord Almighty.
And you became proud and were charming with the beauty of your
face; you committed adultery (and) were prostituted with [s] your 25
grand reputation, you indeed had spread your prostitution to everyone
who passed on their journeys [t]; and you took your garments of finery
and made tattered [u] idols, and you were prostituted upon them. Moreover you shall not enter there, because they did not happen and shall
not take place [v]. And you took the ornaments of glory of gold and 30
silver which were given to you and you made for yourself male, raving
images and were prostituted with them. And the beautiful, fine

---

[d] or : grassy. — [e] lit. cities of the cities. — [16] I adorned you. — [f] lit. fallen. — [g] lit. unfold-
ed. — [h] lit. unclothed. — [i] lit. put to shame (or : exposed naked). — [j] lit. came (or : passed)
(and) reached over you. — [k] lit. you had reached your time. — [l] lit. bloody blood. —
[m] or : excellent (or : varigated) finery. — [17] om. — [18] gave. — [n] i.e. long ear-rings (or :
ear-ring). — [19] om. — [20] om. — [21] om. — [22] garment. — [23] del : om B. — [o] lit. gave. —
[p] or : the kingdom. — [q] lit. name. — [r] or : heathen. — [s] lit. in. — [t] or : roads. — [u] lit.
mended. — [v] or : happen.

garment which I had given to you, with that you adorned them; you offered to them my perfume and splendid ᵂ incense; and you fed them my bread of fine flour which I gave to you and olive oil and honey; and you put all this before them for a sweet odor. And you
5 took your sons and your daughters which you had borne to me (and) sacrificed (these) to them to destruction; and you considered that fornication as (such) a small matter, you killed my children ˣ; this was in fact greater than all your fornications and abominations. And you remembered ʸ the days of your childhood to the time that
10 you were naked (and) bare ᶻ, drenched (and) mixed with blood ᵃᵃ. And there was woe, woe upon woe, says the Lord Almighty. You made for yourself a brothel, a house for your fornications, and you made for yourself idol altars ᵇᵇ in all your public places ᶜᶜ'. More-
⊙ over he says, 'And you were not like ᵈᵈ a prostitute who gathers her
15 price of prostitution, but you were as a wife who commits adultery with her husband ᵉᵉ, who receives treasures from her husband and gives pay ᶠᶠ to her lovers. And all prostitutes receive the price of prostitution for themselves, but you gave pay to your lovers ²⁴'.

68. After these ¹ proclamations ᵃ of the Prophets our new Scrip-
20 tures certified ᵇ, that truly the Church is likened to the bride, and
† Christ to the bridegroom. Even Paul says, 'I betrothed you to one husband as a pure virgin in order to offer ᶜ you to Christ'. And in this manner our ⌐path is ² likened to a betrothal and ³ the preparations ⁴ for a wedding. For when a woman is betrothed to a man, she is ⌐far
25 from him by sight; ⁵ and ⁶ the mediators, ⌐who shall be the match-makers,⁷ remain between (them) and come to the bride; and she hears from them about the greatness of the bridegroom, and about the splendor ⁸ of his beauty, ⌐and about his nobleness ⁹. And by the ears ¹⁰ there, of the matchmakers the love for the bridegroom drops and is sown into
30 the heart of the virgin, and enslaved her mind is carried away with

---

ᵂ or : prepared. — ˣ lit. sons. — ʸ Greek and Hebrew have 'not remembered'. — ᶻ or : shameful. — ᵃᵃ lit. bloody blood. — ᵇᵇ or: temples. — ᶜᶜ or: market-places. — ᵈᵈ lit. you were not in that manner as. — ᵉᵉ lit. man. — ᶠᶠ or : wages. — ²⁴ om.

68. ¹ this. — ᵃ lit. speeches — ᵇ or : affirmed. — ᶜ lit. give — ² paths are. — ³ (and). — ⁴ + of the bride. — ⁵ with sight. — ⁶ by. — ⁷ matchmakers who — ⁸ + and. — ⁹ om. — ¹⁰ hearing.

67. ⊙ Ezk 16:31b-33a.
68. † II Cor 11:2b.

her love [11] for him. And having contemplated [d] she expects to leave her mother who gave birth to her, and her father and her [12] brothers and ⌐their familiar habits; and having contemplated she expects to go out from the house of her nurture [13], in order to go to be joined to (her) husband [e], who [14] with her [15] eyes [f] she had [16] not seen him, but only his [17] name that was mentioned to her. In like manner also we [18], the Apostles were matchmakers for us, and they told us [19] about the greatness [g] of Christ, and about his glories [20], about his great nobleness, and we believed them, and having contemplated [h] we expect to leave this world of our habitation; ⌐and to leave our [21] fathers who begot us, and our [22] mothers who brought us up, our [23] brothers and their familiar habits and to go to be in the presence of Christ, who [24] with our eyes we have not seen him, but only his name that [25] was mentioned to us, and his love ⌐is indeed [26] enflamed in our hearts, and enslaved we are carried away with love [27] for him.

69. As the bridegroom that sends bridal men [a], after they ⌐shall have been [1] clothed with splendid garments, to go to take away the bride from her brothers and from their [2] family [b], and in fact she considers those same bridegroom's men (as) her brothers and sisters, and [3] the bride ⌐indeed confides [4] in [5] them, in like manner also the [6] Lord sends angels of Heaven with glory, in order to ⌐take us away [7] (and) present us to the bridegroom, and we indeed confide in them. And as the bridegroom's men are clothed with fine garments, and are less glorious [c] than their [8] bridegroom, in like manner [9] the Apostles and the angels are clothed with glorious garments [d], nevertheless they are less glorious than Christ. And as the bridegroom, who is himself [10] head of all the ⌐bridegroom's men [11] and the table companions [e] and friends [12], the Apostle says concerning Christ, that 'He himself is the head of all principalities [f] and powers [g]'. As the † virgin [h] works and labors in the house of her father, in order to make

---

[11] + even. — [d]. lit. looked. — [12] om. — [13] om. — [e] lit. man. — [14] + even. — [15] the. — [f] lit. face. — [16] had. — [17] the. — [18] om. — [19] om. — [g] or : riches. — [20] + and. — [h] lit. looked. — [21] om. — [22] om. — [23] om. — [24] + even — [25] om. — [26] is kindled and is. — [27] + which (is).

69. [a] lit. bridegroom's men. — [1] are. — [2] read : 'her' B. — [b] or : kindred. — [3] + she becomes. — [4] om. — [5] for. — [6] our. — [7] see. — [c] lit. smaller with their glory. — [8] the. — [9] + also. — [d] lit. garments of glory. — [10] om. — [11] glorious. — [e] or : guests. — [12] in like manner. — [f] or : sovereignties. — [g] or : authorities. — [h] or : maiden.

69. † Col 2:10b.

her clothes at (her) [13] native home, that she may be pleasing to the bridegroom with them, in like manner also, we labor and work in this world, in which we shall [14] have been born, in order to make (and) prepare ⌐for us [15] good works ⌐in this world [16], that at our rising
5 we also shall be pleasing to Christ ⌐with them [17].

70.   And [1] as the bridegroom is not strange to the virgin who ⌐shall have been [2] betrothed to him because they are of one nature and of one God who has created [a] them, and according to the will of their [3] Creator they are joined to each other; in like manner also we are not
10 strange to our Lord, for ⌐by one God who has created us [4], and according to the will of our Creator we are joined to Christ.   And as it is not proper ⌐for the wife [5] to exchange the bed of her husband with (the bed of) another man, otherwise she is considered an adulteress; in like manner ⌐also we [6], instead of the employment [b] of the bed,
15 God asks from us adoration [c] ⌐and thanksgiving [7], as he also asked from Jerusalem.   And as the wife, as long as she has honorably the [8] husband who was called [d] for her, the modesty of chastity is with her, but if ⌐the wife [9] is troubled in her [10] mind, and she has considered every man as ⌐her husband [11], she shall be called afterwards an adult-
20 eress and a prostitute; not that she has any [12] more affairs [e] with them who are prostituted, but she received them as a [13] husband; in like manner also, as long as we have dread and fear, the worship ⌐of God [14] and adoration for him [15], because ⌐his divinity [16] is indicated to us from the beginning, we also are changed through chastity; but if we [17]
25 turn aside to strange teaching and make other gods, thenceforth we [18] become adulterers and prostitutes.   And in this manner we are compared to the bride, for she goes (and) is joined to the bridegroom. ⌐And as [19] the bride ⌐prepares herself and [20] is adorned [21] with gold ornaments [f,22] and she personally is evidently becoming for the bride-
30 groom, and her clothes with [23] her [24] finery [g] make her pleasing in

---

[13] her. — [14] om. — [15] om. — [16] om. — [17] om.

70.   [1] om. — [2] was. — [a] or : confirmed. — [3] the. — [4] from our created nature we have received a body, true, intelligent and reasonable, and indeed united with an in-dissoluble union with his uncreated, divine nature with the concurrence of the Father and the Holy Spirit. — [5] om. — [6] om. — [b] or : service. — [c] or : worship. — [7] om. — [8] her. — [d] or : named. — [9] she. — [10] om. — [11] hers. — [12] om. — [e] lit. does any more works. — [13] her. — [14] om. — [15] God. — [16] worship of him. — [17] + shall. — [18] + also. — [19] om. — [20] om. — [21] + with garments and. — [f] or : finery. — [22] om. — [23] and. — [24] om. — [g] or : ornaments.

the presence of her [25] bridegroom, and [26] she is evidently becoming
to him ⌜for his needs [27], and he is completely happy with (his) wife,
in like manner also, our good and righteous works become to us [28]
clothes [29], as ⌜dressed with [30] finery that we may be pleasing to our [31]
Lord with them. And ⌜in fact [32] we personally are becoming to [5]
Christ, for he himself is the bridegroom.

71. And as a woman when she adorns herself, does not go (and)
inquire to one of her companions whether she ⌜may be [1] beautiful
or not, nor does she [2] believe ⌜anyone concerning [3] her finery, whether
it is becoming to her, but [4] she takes her mirror and looks at herself [10]
and[5] is happy ⌜with herself [6] in her finery, and she knows [7] ⌜that she
shall be pleasing [8] for herself [9], then she shall [10] be pleasing also [11]
to the bridegroom, to whom she is going. And if there shall be any
spot [12] ⌜on the front of [13] her face, or any ⌜color of [14] stain, or wrink-
le [a,15], she cleans (and) clears it; and she adorns herself, so that she [15]
shall be pleasing to the bridegroom [16]. ⌜In like manner also we, for
we are betrothed to Christ the bridegroom [17], and ⌜no one knows [18]
whether we ⌜may be [19] beautiful or ugly, unless we take in (our) hand
the Holy [20] Scriptures in the form of a mirror; and having looked
we [21] examine ourselves, and [22] if we with our [23] works shall be good [20]
to ourselves [b], we also shall be likened to the living commandments;
⌜for they [24] are the mirror, then we also shall be [25] good [c] to our Lord.
And as it is not possible in the world that anyone who indeed sees
his face, shall also succeed [d] in the presence of it to see ⌜in it [26] the
beauty and [27] the ugliness of himself [28], except only [29] by means of [25]
a mirror; in like manner there is no one in the world who is able to
see the image [30] of himself, whether his works ⌜shall be ugly [31] or
beautiful [32], but every man appears good in his own eyes. But when
we take in (our) hands the mirror of the Holy Scriptures, we do not
embellish [e] ourselves as our minds ⌜shall suppose [33] that we ⌜shall [30]

---

[25] om. — [26] moreover. — [27] om. — [28] + as. — [29] + and. — [30] om. — [31] the. — [32] om.
    71. [1] is. — [2] + first. — [3] about. — [4] until. — [5] + then. — [6] om. — [7] shall know. —
[8] the satisfaction. — [9] + and. — [10] + indeed. — [11] om. — [12] spots. — [13] of color on. —
[14] om. — [a] lit. corner of wrinkling. — [15] corner of wrinkling. — [16] + Christ. — [17] om. —
[18] one knows not. — [19] are. — [20] om. — [21] add. : 'shall' B. — [22] om. — [23] good. — [b] i.e.
seem good to ourselves. — [24] which. — [25] + considered. — [c] i.e. shall seem good. —
[d] lit. be successful. — [26] om. — [27] or. — [28] his face. — [29] om. — [30] ugliness. — [31] are bad.
— [32] good. — [e] lit. adorn. — [33] supposed.

have been [34] good, ⌜but as [35] our [36] Scriptures show (us) [37] ⌜with the
† image in the mirror [38]; for [39] the Apostle says, 'Now we see the glory
of the Lord [40] by an example ⌜as with [41] a mirror', and we resemble
to the same image. As much as we look into the Scriptures [42], there
5 is in them, the power to put our images before our faces [43]. And
⌜they shall be [44] for us a mirror, and [45] ⌜he shall be [46] happy ⌜with
our [47] good condition [f,48], and he ⌜shall clean [49] and take [50] away
from us the evil stains and spots [g] of impurity, and when our
minds know that ⌜we shall be [h] good to ourselves [51], as the mirror of
10 our [52] Scriptures shows us, then we know that we shall be pleasing to
the Lord; and [53] he is happy with us, as the bridegroom ⌜is happy[54]
with the bride, ⌜as she is [55] in no way at all imperfect [i].

72. Moreover, ⌜they who shall be [1] the bridal mediators, they
tell the bride about the greatness of the bridegroom, and [2] about
15 his reputation [a] and about his ⌜nobleness and [3] power. In like manner
also they praise [4] the bride before the bridegroom, and ⌜they tell
him about the beautiful disposition of the virgin [b] whom they betrothed [c] to him [5], and about her chastity, and about [6] her good
condition [d]. And when ⌜the bride [7] goes (and) is united with the
20 bridegroom and [8] he is happy with her, afterwards she possesses
his property, and she becomes partaker of [e] his glory. Moreover the
matchmakers who shall be the mediators are seated [9] in the wedding
chamber [f], and they are happy ⌜with the bride [10] and with the bridegroom, when the crown of glory is placed on their heads [g], and they
25 ⌜shall be [11] happy at the wedding [12]. For while the bride was afar off
from the bridegroom, they taught her the desires of the bridegroom;
when she saw the bridegroom [13], she was happy ⌜with him, and [14]
the words of the mediator were indeed confirmed; and from the

---

34 (are). — 35 thus. — 36 the mirror of the. — 37 us. — 38 the same (thing). — 39 and. —
40 + as. — 41 of. — 42 + since. — 43 eyes. — 44 when they are. — 45 om. — 46 we are.—
47 in. — f lit. order. — 48 works. — 49 cleans. — 50 takes. — g or: blemishes. — h i.e.
seem. — 51 (we) ourselves are good. — 52 Holy. — 53 om. — 54 om. — 55 by having found
us. — i lit. in need.

72. 1 om. — 2 om. — a lit. name. — 3 noble. — 4 speak about. — b or : maiden. —
c or : spoke of. — 5 the beauty of the bride, which they saw in her, they praise. — 6 om.
— d lit. order. — 7 she. — 8 om. — e or : partner to. — 9 + with him. — f lit. curtain.
— 10 at the wedding. — g i.e. they are married. — 11 are. — 12 + feast. — 13 + and. —
14 om.

71. † I Cor 13:12a

bridegroom there appears [15] the honor ⌜of praises [16] for them. In like manner also, the Apostles became for us the matchmakers and approachers, and they told us about ⌜the greatness and [17] the honor of the praises of our Lord; and they offered to him the good words, and with their prayers they offered [18] reconciliation and our suppli- ⁵ cations [19] before the Most High, and they showed us all the desires [h] of our Lord; if we learn chastity and [20] modesty and [21] holiness and all the desires of the bridegroom, when we go (and) are joined to him he is happy with us, and from him there appears the honor of praises for the Apostles, for they instructed us and taught ⌜us the things [22] ¹⁰ of the bridegroom, and presented [23] offerings ⌜of joy [24] for us, and ⌜they were honored on account of [25] us. For [26] Paul himself bears witness and says, 'What recompense shall there be for us, or joy, † or crown of glory, unless you (are) before our Lord Jesus Christ at his coming ?'. ¹⁵

73. For [1] concerning all this the Law itself bears witness, for it is written in the Book of Genesis at the time when they betrothed Rebecca to Isaac; Abraham called the eldest [a] of his servants, and [2] he himself was [3] his steward [b], and he says to him: 'Bring ⌜(and) put † your hand [4] under my thigh, and swear ⌜to me [5] by the Lord God ²⁰ whose are the heavens and the earth, that you shall not take a wife for my son ⌜of the daughters of the Canaanites [6], among whom I have settled at present, but go to my country and to my heritage, and there you shall take a wife to my son Isaac'. The peace of God had [7] dwelt in the land of the Canaanites and the inhabitants of the land ²⁵ were [8] wicked and unjust; therefore Abraham took the oath with the eldest [c] of his servants, and he says: 'Take not a wife for my son ⊙ from this land'. However because Isaac [9] blessed God [10], because they [11] shall be the lord of that land, Abraham commanded that he shall not take a wife for Isaac from the wicked men, for [12] the evil ³⁰

---

[15] shall appear. — [16] om. — [17] om. — [18] + us for. — [19] + they offered. — [h] lit. wills. — [20] om. — [21] om. — [22] the will. — [23] + joyful. — [24] om. — [25] because they reported for. — [26] om.

73. [1] And. — [a] or : elder. — [2] who. — [3] is. — [b] or : manager. — [4] your hand and put (it). — [5] om. — [6] om. — [7] has. — [8] are. — [c] or : elder. — [9] God. — [10] Isaac. — [11] he. — [12] lest. —

72. † I Thess 2:19.
73. † Gen 24:2b-4. 73. ⊙ Allusion to Gen 24:3b.

woman and her children would inherit the good land; but that one
who shall be worthy, she shall come from the distant land, and from
the impure land, for she shall be the wife for the son who was born
according to the promise ᵈ, and he shall become king over the good
5 land.   In like manner the peace of the Lord ¹³ God had dwelt in the
House ¹⁴ of Israel, but ᵉ they were not worthy to be united and joined
to Christ because of their wickedness.   However the Word of our
Lord was sent by means of his Apostles that they might persuade
and bring the people, that those, who are from the heathens from the
10 impure ᶠ land ⌐and are ¹⁵ in the likeness of a wife, ⌐might come (and) ¹⁶
be joined to Christ, who has been born according to the promise and
he shall be king over the inheritance of life.

† 74.   The ⌐eldest of his servants ¹ says to ⌐his master ², 'Master,
if the woman shall not want to come ³ with me, do I indeed return
⊙ your son?'.   Abraham says to his servant, 'If the woman does not
wish to follow you, you shall be innocent ᵃ from this oath, but only
you shall not bring my son thither'.   For if the eldest of the servants
shall not go to persuade the woman from the distant land, he will
be bound to severe punishment by his master.   But if he shall go,
20 and the woman shall not ⌐want (to come) ⁴, the woman shall indeed
become forsaken from the inheritance to which she was called, and
the servant is freed from severe punishment.   In like manner also
our people are ⁵ from the heathens, for these were called to go to
inherit the inheritance which shall never have been seen by them; if
25 we are persuaded to follow our matchmaker Apostles, we shall approach
and shall be joined to the children of promise and ⁶ to the Blessed
Bridegroom, and we shall inherit the Kingdom which will have never
been seen by us; and our persuasive Apostles receive praise and honor.
But if they indeed would have been afraid and would not go to preach
30 and to call us, they would be bound to severe punishment; as also
● the Apostle says, 'Woe is unto me, if I shall not preach the Gospel'.
But if they shall come to us and we will not go, they are freed from

---

ᵈ lit. good news. — ¹³ om. — ¹⁴ + of the God. — ᵉ lit. and. — ᶠ or : unclean. — ¹⁵ om. —
¹⁶ having come, might.

74.   ¹ servant. — ² Abraham. — ³ read : 'follow' B. — ᵃ lit. expiated. — ⁴ come. —
⁵ om. — ⁶ om.

74.   † Gen 24:5. — ⊙ Gen 24:8. — ● I Cor 9:16c.

severe punishment, and we become forsaken [b] and unprovided [c] from
the inheritance to [7] which we were called, and Christ comes not (nor)
is joined to us or dwells with us, as also the command the servant
received from Abraham, says, 'You shall not return my son thither'. ⸗

75. While the servant was going on the road, he supplicated [5]
God and prayed that with love and willingly [a] he might know the
woman for whom he had come, as previously [b] was promised seriously
to be before him, and to diligently give an answer, for in this manner
he spoke, 'O Lord God of my master Abraham, if you would make †
prosperous my journey before me today, let it happen to me (that) [10]
when I ⌜shall see [1] a virgin [c] on this well and shall say to her, 'Give
to me a little water to drink', and she shall say to me, 'Drink, and
give to your camels ⌜so that they might drink [2]' — let this [3] be the
woman who shall be prepared by the Lord God for his [4] servant
Isaac'. In like manner also, as we were elected [d] before coming [e] [15]
into the world, (as) they who listened to the Apostles with love and
willingly [5], with joy and consistence, when we stand before our Gospel
writers, at that time we are presented to the glorified Bridegroom.

76. Even as [1] the eldest of the servants came, he found there
a gentle, discreet maiden, and the water pot (was) on her shoulder, [20]
and he said [a] to her, 'Give to me [2] water from that place ⌜to drink [3]'.
And she quickly hastened (and) lowered the pitcher, bent down her
arms and said [b], 'You also drink and your camels'. And as he drank
and gave to the camels, he said [c] to her, 'Whose daughter are you',
and [4] she said [d] to him, 'I am the daughter of Bethuel the son of [25]
Nahor, who was born to him of Milcah [5]'. He said [e] to her, 'Is there
in your house a place ⌜for us [6] for lodging?'. And she said [f] to him,
'There is plenty food for the animals at our house, and ample place
for lodging'. And the servant took bracelets, (and) [7] put (them) on
the arms of the girl, and ear-rings on her ears; there on the water [30]
fountain. In like manner also at the fountain of baptism we are

---

[b] lit. impoverished. — [c] lit. needy. — [7] from.

75.   [a] or : voluntarily. — [b] lit. before the time. — [1] have seen. — [c] or : maiden. —
[2] to drink. — [3] that. — [4] the. — [d] or : chosen. — [e] lit. being. — [5] + and.

76.   [1] + bridal men. — [a] lit. says. — [2] + of the. — [3] om. — [b] lit says. — [c] lit. says. —
[4] om. — [d] lit. says. — [5] + And. — [e] lit. says. — [6] om. — [f] lit. says. — [7] and.

74.   ⸗ Gen 24:8b.
75.   † Gen 24:12ff (Paraphrase).

betrothed, with the Apostles for our matchmakers, and by baptism
we receive the ornament of good works in the likeness of gold [8] and
precious gems. And this is clear to us that the eldest of the servants
who was the steward [g] for Abraham, came to Bethuel the father of
5 Rebecca and to Laban her brother, not [h] to be fed and that he might
receive him, but that he might take the girl and carry (her) to the good
inheritance. However it was necessary to the affairs and was proper
first [9] to receive him and his animals at the house there in which the
bride was brought up; and then having taken her away, she is carried
10 to the great and honorable inheritance. In like manner also in the
time when our Lord sent the twelve Apostles in order to preach [1] to
every man eternal life, and to call the people from the world to
heaven [10], ⌜even he, gave the command to them [11].

†   77. The more so our Lord says, 'He who wants to be my disciple,
15 unless he is separated from all his possessions, he can not be my
disciple'; however that [1] also he taught (them) by the first prophets,
that they shall have [a] disciples. And they learned [2] their ways and
the modesty of their wisdom and their thoughts about poverty and
the monastic life [b], which was in ⌜their teacher's [3] worship of God [c].
20 When [4] the thoughts and example of our Savior were preached to [5]
them and he came and accomplished [d] their thoughts and ways
which were on account of him, and [6] their words ⌜which were on account
of him [7] were verified and sealed ⌜to their hearers [8]. Even our Savior
himself taught nothing [9] from his mind, but he taught according to
⊙ the will of his Father, as also he says, 'The Son speaks not [10] his own

---

[8] + and silver. — [g] or : manager. — [h] or : not only. — [9] om. — [1] lit. preach the Gospel. — [10] +
he says, 'whatever they put before you eat, for the laborer is worthy of his food' (I Cor
10:27b + Mt 10:10b); and thus he taught the disciples to feed the animals as well as
their bodies; not that by feeding they are changed, but that it might lead them from
earth to heaven to the marriage. Nevertheless it is very necessary according to the
writing of Paul, 'Who would pasture sheep and would not drink from the milk, or would
plant a vineyard and would not taste of the fruit ? Which also the law expressed with the
proverb, 'You shall not bind the mouth of the ox which treads the threshing-floor' : for
not that the animal, but for us it was written, who for the spiritual we confirm among
you grace'. (I Cor 9:7b-11). Now thus according to the parables and prophecies (i.e.
the writing of the prophets) of the Scriptures our Lord was likened to a bridegroom and
the people of his Church to the bride. — [11] om.

    77.   [1] this. — [a] lit. there shall be for them — [2] shall learn. — [b] or : solitude — [3] the. —
[c] or : religious devotion — [4] For. — [5] by. — [d] or : fulfilled — [6] + thus. — [7] om. — [8] om.
— [9] not. — [10] + according to.

    77.   † Lk 14:33. ⊙ Allusion to Jn 8:28 (see also Jn 5:19,30; 6:38; 14:10).

will, but whatever he sees and hears from his [11] Father, that he speaks'.
For this reason : lest anyone might think that our Lord spoke anything
from himself.   For [12] the example and thoughts, which were on account
of him, and the figures of the forms of his works, through which also [13]
the Prophets worked ⌜everything which was on account of him [14], 5
he came [15], accomplished and [16] sealed them to his hearers.

78.   Now let us fear his powerful and severe Father, ⌜as also the
Scriptures say [1], 'It is a great fear to fall into the hands of the living †
God', for he himself works through his Son all that he wills.   Therefore
as our Savior himself and his Prophets and Apostles were separated 10
from the world through their [2] worship of God and their [3] wisdom
and their spiritual ways, and through their habits [a], and through
their eating and drinking, and through their glorified words [4], in like
manner also let us be imitators of our Teacher and of our partners,
his first disciples ; for [5] our souls should be separated from the world 15
through the worship of God and through wisdom, and through habits
in the world, ⌜and through eating and drinking [6] and through spiritual
conduct ; and do not be confused between the words and worldly
talk ; for if through our conduct and habits and eating and drinking
and our words we are not separated and we are not divided from 20
wordly men ; ⌜if then it will be thus [7], then to the winds and to the
stones our Lord came (and) spoke the glorious commandments [8]
from his Father, and he was not sent to us personnally, or perhaps
the throne of his greatness (is) terrible (and) [9] violent, when his Father
directs according to his will, he judges the winds and the stones, and 25
⌜he does not judge us personally [10].

79.   Let us come then and do [1] that which the [2] Savior recommended
to us of the will of his Father, for [3] God is a burning [4] fire, as also the
Scriptures say.   If anyone applies to himself the name of discipleship,
and he is not worthy of it, he shall be regarded with Gehazi, the disciple 30
of Elisha who appropriated [a] the name, and he did not in effect fulfill

---

[11] om. — [12] But. — [13] om. — [14] om. — [15] + and having. — [16] om.

78.   [1] om. — [2] the. — [3] om. — [a] or : habitations. — [4] conduct. — [5] according to
whom. — [6] om. — [7] thus. — [8] + which (are). — [9] and. — [10] not us.

79.   [1] say. — [2] our. — [3] + our. — [4] combustive. — [a] lit. was joined with.

78.   † Heb 10:31.

(it). For he abandoned the heavenly ᵇ possessions and he desired ⁵
worldly possessions ⁶, therefore he was rejected and he took ᶜ on
leprosy. And moreover he shall be regarded with Judas, who was
one in the number of the twelve ⌜Apostles of our Savior ⁷; since he
₅ desired of the possessions of the world, he also was rejected and ⌜his
name ⁸ was erased from the list of life.

80. Now let us ⌜be afraid of ¹ this world and its goods, so that
we ⌜also shall not ² be rejected ⌜and fallen ³ from the place ᵃ in which
we stand, as also they in fact were rejected. For ⌜to oppose and
₁₀ resist against the discipleship, this is ⁴ envy and greed, and all desires
of the world. ⌜And these in fact ⁵ subverted ᵇ the wise and the strong
giants, and it removes many from the kingdom in that day; for
they are the weapon of the enemy ⁶, for ⁷ through them he fights ᶜ
with us, therefore our Lord stripped ⌜(and) removed ⁸ his weapon
† and delivered ᵈ us, for he said ⌜to us ⁹, 'He who ⌜will be ¹⁰ my servant ᵉ,
let him follow me'. Therefore we follow him, and we are imitators
of his conduct, and we put it on as a weapon ᶠ; for our Savior ¹¹ knows
the ⌜cunning ᵍ of the hypocrisy ¹² of Satan, for he agitates and disturbs
the men who believe, so that he fraudulently deceives ¹³ some through
₂₀ possessions and goods, and through many other things, so that this
might subvert him ¹⁴; and sometimes he sees someone that is clothed
with armor, (and) he makes war with him ¹⁵ and ¹⁶ with the thoughts
of the Scriptures ¹⁷, ⌜that he might break ¹⁸ (his) vow and ⌜subvert
him ¹⁹; and it is because one from the lists of ²⁰ teachings deposes
₂₅ him. Therefore our Lord pitied ʰ us when he said that we should
keep his commandments; and the grace of his mercy shall come (and)
reach us, to deliver us from evil; for when (we) keep his commandments we escape from Satan who makes war with us in diverse ways;
and the Holy Spirit hovers over us, ⌜as also over the Prophets ²¹.
₃₀ 81. Now let us liken to our Teacher and the Prophets and the
Apostles whom we were founded upon, they who wore the armor of

---

ᵇ or : divine. — ⁵ loved the. — ⁶ om. — ᶜ lit. put. — ⁷ disciples of our Lord. — ⁸ he.

80. ¹ flee from. — ² never shall. — ³ om. — ᵃ or : rank. — ⁴ om. — ⁵ they. — ᵇ or :
overthrew. — ⁶ devil. — ⁷ and. — ᶜ lit. makes war. — ⁸ om. — ᵈ lit. gave. — ⁹ om. —
¹⁰ is. — ᵉ or : minister. — ᶠ or : armor. — ¹¹ Lord. — ᵍ or : deceit. — ¹² hypocrisy of the
cunning. — ¹³ besets. — ¹⁴ read : 'them' B. — ¹⁵ them. — ¹⁶ om. — ¹⁷ + having fought. —
¹⁸ he breaks. — ¹⁹ subverts them. — ²⁰ + heretical. — ʰ or : pardoned. — ²¹ om.

80.   † Jn 12:26a.

their Lord and overcame the enemy [1]; moreover the blessed Paul
says, 'I wish, brethren, that you would be imitators of me'.   Where- †
fore, he says, 'I desired not gold and [2] silver, nor fine [a] clothes, but ⊙
I loved to labor with my hands and to feed and to give also to the
weak ⌐in need [3]'; moreover he [4] showed that by those ways we should 5
walk.   And moreover as the [5] Apostles, whatever ⌐there was for
them [6], they brought that into (their) midst, and no one among them
was poor, for all persons are equal with their home and love [7].   But
if we do not listen to Paul and we do not obey our Savior, ⌐we do not
become imitators of the Prophets and the Apostles [8].   Then [9] let us 10
not despise [b] the words of Holy Scripture because of our weakness,
for the Word of [10] God is yea, yea and nay, nay; as also Paul says,
'The Word of God is living [c], and it is sharper than every two edged ᴐ
sword, cutting through ⌐(and) reaching [11] to the separation of spirit
and body, to the joints and shanks; and he is the judge [d] ⌐of the 15
thoughts and intentions [12] of the [13] heart; and there is no created
thing which ⌐is hidden [14] from him, but everything is manifest before
him, for we are standing naked [e] before ⌐his face [15], ⌐to whom [16] each
one of us is to give account'.   This example of the discipleship of
which our Lord spoke, he spoke for the sake of perfection [f], for he 20
who wants [17] to be perfected [g] should be [18] like [19] this [20].

   82.   ⌐The more so [1], Paul says, 'As to babes in Christ I fed you †
milk, and ⌐I did not give you [2] solid food, because at this time you
are yet carnal [a]; ⌐for you were not able to receive (it) while you are
carnal'; and moreover [3] ⌐he says [4], 'The solid food is for the perfected, ⊙
⌐for those [5] whose senses are trained, to distinguish evil and good'.
⌐And in this manner, this which he says (is) true, 'As to babes in ᴐ

81.   [1] devil. — [2] or. — [a] lit. delicate. — [3] and needy, 'behold. — [4] + also. — [5] +
first. — [6] they had. — [7] + Thus we ought to have equality with our possessions to the
poor and to the needy brethren. — [8] we inherit perdition. — [9] Nevertheless. — [b] lit.
put under foot. — [10] + our. — [c] or : alive, sprightly. — [11] del : om B. — [d] or : discerner.
— [12] om. — [13] all. — [14] is able to hide. — [e] or : open. — [15] him. — [16] om. — [f] or : maturity.
— [17] read : 'shall want' B. — [g] or : matured. — [18] remain. — [19] + all. — [20] + to re-
nounce all (things) and with the cross to follow him, according to the absolute purpose
of the desire for perfecting (one's) condition.
   82.   [1] Moreover that which. — [2] not. — [a] lit. with the flesh. — [3] om. — [4] and. —
[5] del : om B.

81.   † Gal 4:12. — ⊙ Acts 20:33-35a. — ᴐ Heb 4:12,13.
82.   † I Cor 3:1c-3a. — ⊙ Heb 5:14 — ᴐ I Cor 3:1c-2a.

Christ I fed you milk ⁶', for as a babe at first sucks milk, and with
that it is brought up and little by little it grows stronger on the nourishment of the tastes of meat ᵇ, and it begins to distinguish the good
and the evil ⌐and the sweet from the bitter ⁷ and then it advances
⁵ to eat meat with bread ᶜ and everything as a man, and he forgets
⌐his childhood (and) ⁸ the milk which was ⁹ sucked in his infancy
for the strength of his force, and ¹⁰ because ⌐with meats ¹¹ he was
perfected to the measure of his ¹² being which God confirmed in him,
in like manner also we in the likeness of the milk study the first books,
¹⁰ and with them we are brought up, and little by little our faith ⌐and
worship of our Lord ¹³ grows stronger in us, and then we begin to
understand ¹⁴, to distinguish the good and the evil and the sweet from
the bitter ¹⁵.   When our faith ¹⁶ becomes confirmed in ⌐its intensity,
and then with our involuntary wills our minds drive ᵈ us ¹⁷ to the
¹⁵ perfection of the truth of the Gospels, for they themselves are the
ȸ solid foods, as also ¹⁸ the Apostle says, ⌐'The solid food is for the
☐ perfected ¹⁹'.   For this reason moreover ²⁰ the Apostle said ²¹, 'As to
babes in Christ I fed you milk'.   Though at first as milk we drank
the instruction of the teaching, when we are perfected ᵉ and are
²⁰ confirmed in it, in that time we indeed approach to the commandments
of the Gospels, and ²² they themselves are the perfection of the stature
of the perfected ⌐and solid food ²³.
†   83.   The more so moreover ¹, says our Lord, 'Endeavor to enter
at the narrow door'.   And we see this same thing that the door of
²⁵ the Kingdom ⌐shall be ² in this manner ³.   He who indeed ⁴ desires
to enlist and write himself on the list ⌐of the number ⁵ of the soldiers
here on earth, first puts this on his mind: to leave his house and his
kindred, in order ⌐for him ⁶ to go away to other regions ⌐and for him ⁷
to battle ᵃ to death ⁸.   As ⌐a soldier ⁹, he first learns (how) to cleanse
³⁰ and polish his armor, and learns the things of war when he shall be

---

⁶ om. — ᵇ or : food. — ⁷ om. — ᶜ or : the food of bread. — ⁸ om. — ⁹ he. — ¹⁰ om. —
¹¹ om. — ¹² om. — ¹³ om. — ¹⁴ + and. — ¹⁵ + Moreover. — ¹⁶ minds. — ᵈ lit. throw. —
¹⁷ the worship of our Lord and his wisdom, then in his condescension our minds take us
in wisdom. — ¹⁸ om. — ¹⁹ and. — ²⁰ om. — ²¹ + that. — ᵉ or : matured. — ²² for. —
²³ om.

   83.   ¹ om. — ² was. — ³ + For. — ⁴ om. — ⁵ om. — ⁶ also. — ⁷ om. — ᵃ lit. undertake
war. — ⁸ + And. — ⁹ the rank of soldiers.

   82.   ȸ Heb 5:14a — ☐ I Cor 3 : Ic-2a
   83.   † Lk 13:24a.

specifically alone; before the time of war shall have arrived [b,10],
he joins [c] with the armed warriors; and he sees nothing else there,
but the brightness of the armor, and the glitter of the sword, and the
bravery of the horsemen, and the whizzing [d] of the bows; and ⌈he
hears [11] nothing else there, but the sound of the harp being struck, 5
and the ringing of the trumpets [e,12], and the ⌈urging of the flute,
the terror of the sword and the encouragement of the trumpets [13].
Some [f] bleed [g]; and some when they hear the sound of the terrible
clamor, having fallen they are indeed exhausted from their [14] fright;
and some having been encouraged grow stronger, and they take 10
courage from them and their fellow-comrades; and some raise their
eyes and see that the sword (is) in front of them and behind them,
and say in their minds, 'If we are indeed weakened in this war, before
us the ⌈sword will kill [15] us, and if we shall turn back [16], they who
shall be ours will beat (us) with rods, but I will die like a man', and 15
they raise their eyes to heaven and [17] call to God with prayers, and
they give themselves to the battle like men.　This is what our ⌈Savior-
Redeemer [18] said, ⌈he says [19], 'He who joins me, joins with fire, and ⊙
he [20] who is [21] far ⌈from me [22] is [23] far from life'.　In like manner also,
we who desired the heavenly door of the kingdom and shall be written [24] 20
in the lists of life with the soldiers, with the Prophets, with the Apostles,
at first we shall [25] learn the things of war: the commandments and
the laws of our Lord, and with them we instruct ourselves every day,
and we ⌈are cleansed [26] as the armor, and we are confirmed in our
hearts, and then we wear them as armor [27], thenceforth we are brave 25
and powerful ⌈to oppose [28] in war ⌈since we shall have been clothed
with them [29].

[b] text is corrupt here, see Codex B. — [10] add : 'every day he takes care of his things;
and when the day of battle comes (and) arrives' B. — [c] lit. falls among. — [d] or ,
humming. — [11] they hear. — [e] or : horns. — [12] trumpet. — [13] the beat of the drum,
the alarming encouragement of the songs. — [f] 'some' is singular in Armenian. — [g] lit.
pass forward blood. — [14] om. — [15] swords kill. — [16] our backs. — [17] (and). — [18] Lord.
— [19] om. — [20] they. — [21] shall be. — [22] om. — [23] are. — [24] numbered. — [25] om. —
[26] wear. — [27] + and. — [28] om. — [29] after we have been instructed of them, with the
knowledge of soldiership.

83.　⊙ Agraphon — see Origen's Commentary on Jeremiah 20:3, and Didymus of
Alexandria on Psalms 88:8; cf. John Rylands Library Bulletin, No. 8, 1924, p. 22.

84. But if we are not clothed with this [1] armor, when there is [2] war ⌐or persecution [3], or any other adversity ⌐shall rise [4] against [a] us — for our war is daily and [5] we should [6] have the [7] armor of faith — and [8] when Satan ⌐approaches to any one of us [9] ⌐in order to make 5 war [10] against him [11], some deny [b] ⌐in fear, and [12] have not the armor of faith; and [13] some hear the sound of the trumpet, for it urges, and having been encouraged they grow stronger in order to oppose; and some are asleep and are not watchful, and have a vow to God and are not firm to it, for (they) consider strange, vain ministers [14] 10 of God. And all these persons are written on the lists [c] of the number of the soldiers for the call of the Gospels ⌐and they were overcome [d] † by Satan [15]. In like manner also Paul spoke [16], he says, 'For us the battle is not with flesh [e] and blood, but with principalities [17], and with the world [18] ⌐rulers of this darkness, ⌐who (are) under heaven [f], 15 and with these spirits of perversion [19]'.

85. And as the soldier who is [1] enlisted, from (his) smallness he attains to ⌐greatness of [2] dignity because of his [3] battles [a] and his services [b] of bravery, and ⌐because of his disposition; for with devotion [4] he stands before the king [5], ⌐and he [6] receives ⌐from him [7] very 20 great gifts [8] : praises and ⌐honors and greatness [9], and he indeed is raised in his [10] dignity [c], ⌐and he stands at the royal door [11], and having fed delicately he becomes delicate [d] ⌐in the house of greatness [12]; in like manner also, we are called in [e] littleness and we attain [13] to greatness because of our war-services, and ⌐our war-braveries [14] 25 ⌐and our devotion [15], and we stand before the Heavenly King and receive from him ⌐very great gifts [16]: praises and honor and greatness, and we indeed are raised in dignity with the Prophets and Apostles, ⌐and we become great and rise, and we stand before the Heavenly

---

84. [1] om. — [2] shall be. — [3] om. — [4] om. — [a] lit. over. — [5] + if. — [6] + not. — [7] this. — [8] om. — [9] om. — [10] makes war. — [11] us. — [b] or : disavow. — [12] for. — [13] om. — [14] worship. — [c] or : number. — [d] or : conquered. — [15] om. — [16] om. — [e] lit. body. — [17] add : 'and with powers' B. — [18] om. — [f] lit. in the heavens. — [19] read : 'with these spirits of wickedness which are under heaven' B.

85. [1] (is). — [2] om. — [3] the. — [a] lit. wars. — [b] lit. labor. — [4] having excelled. — [5] + thenceforth, having become proud with valor. — [6] by which he also. — [7] om. — [8] + and. — [9] honor. — [10] om. — [c] or : rank. — [11] om. — [d] lit. soft (or : nice). — [12] at the royal door. — [e] lit. with. — [13] are confirmed. — [14] war bravery. — [15] om. — [16] om. —

84. † Eph. 6:12.

King [17], and having fed delicately we become delicate in the heavenly [18] house ⌐of greatness [19].

86.   And moreover the more so our Lord said, he says, 'The King- †
dom of Heaven is likened to a merchant man who searches [1] for an
excellent pearl [2]; and [3] he found an ⌐excellent and costly [4] pearl; 5
he went (and) sold his everything, and he bought it'.   And moreover
he spoke this to [5] the complete discipleship; for he himself is the
pearl and we (are) the merchants who found him.   And as the excellent
pearl that makes the heart joyful and lifts up the mind ⌐and spirit
and body [6] of him who has it, and makes him becoming and handsome 10
and (is) [7] lifted up in his mind, in like manner also, if we possess the
pearl of our Lord, ⌐that is, the commandments [8], one becomes joyful
⌐and it rejoices his soul and spirit [9], and ⌐his heart [10] becomes joyful
within [11], and having become handsome we are becoming ⌐in ourselves [12] through our pearl [13] which is [14] within us.   And as they do 15
not put the excellent and costly pearl carelessly (and) vainly into the
treasury of the kingdom, but having bound (and) wrapped (it) up
with many seals, they put it [15] in keeping with a large guard [a]; in like
manner also, our pearl having wrapped up, bound ⌐and sealed [16] (it)
with various seals, it has been put [17] in our hearts in keeping with 20
great precaution; and the worship of God our Lord remains (and) is
kept in the [18] heart and the soul and the spirit.

87.   And moreover the more so our Lord says, 'The Kingdom of †
Heaven is likened to a man who found a treasure in a field; and from
his joy he went (and) sold [1], and bought it'.   And moreover he spoke 25
this for the complete discipleship, for he himself is the treasure which
his Father arranged [2] for us.   But as when ⌐we find [3] treasure, it
was not only treasured up at the time in which he found it, ⌐but in fact
it was treasured up in ancient times, and according to the will of
God he found [4] that which he found.   Therefore [5] the treasure is 30

---

[17] om. — [18] royal. — [19] om.

86.   [1] read : 'was searching' B. — [2] read : 'pearls' B. — [3] om. — [4] costly and excellent.
— [5] for. — [6] om. — [7] is. — [8] om. — [9] om. — [10] our souls. — [11] om. — [12] om. — [13] pearls. —
[14] shall be. — [15] om. — [a] or : great precaution. — [16] om. — [17] om. — [18] our.

87.   [1] add : 'his everything' B. — [2] read : 'treasured up' B. — [3] he finds. — [4] om. —
[5] And now.

86.   † Mt 13:45,46.
87.   † Mt 13:44 (condensed paraphrase).

our Savior and not what even now we have found, as the Marcionites
say, but he had been treasured up (and) placed by his Father in ancient
times, and he did not reveal (it) [6] to those nations which were hoping
and were waiting for him, but ⌐he revealed it [7] to us to our nation
5 here; therefore, he was compared to the treasure and the pearl [8]
and we to its finder, according to the will of our Creator [9]. And as
concerning treasure, ⌐he has not only one [10] treasure or riches, ⌐but
he has many treasures and riches [11]; when one discovers that which
he finds, he indeed is astonished and indeed hastens himself, and
10 there is mixed up with the joy in his heart, fear and dread, and his
eyes indeed carefully [12] look about to this side and that side, and he
lifts up his eyes to the heavens; and bread nor water is necessary for
him from the anxiety [a] and labors and sleeplessness ⌐of his joys [13],
for his [14] discoveries which he found are [15] greater than himself. In
15 like manner also our Savior who revealed to us his Father [16], disclosed
⌐with his mouth the [17] treasures of joys, and [18] he produced from
him not only one riches and treasure but many riches and treasures.
And when having been settled we will [19] carry with ⌐our minds [20]
the riches and treasures of his Father, our hearts are indeed astonished
20 by the pleasure ⌐of his joys [21], for there is mixed up ⌐with it [22] fear
and dread because of the riches we found; and with labor and sleeplessness and anxieties, by day and by night, we are anxious about
our treasure; and we do not feel hungry or thirsty, and our eyes are
always lifted to the heavens.

† 88. Moreover, the more so our Lord said [1], ⌐he says [2], 'When anyone
shall invite you to weddings or feasts, do not go (and) sit down at the
highest place lest there should come (and) enter to the host a man
more honorable than you, and that [3] one who shall have invited
both you and him, shall come and shall say, 'Arise, make a place for
30 this one'; and then with shame you shall be presented to a lower
place. However when ⌐they shall invite you [4], go (and) sit down at

[6] it. — [7] it was revealed. — [8] + now he who finds the treasure moves his eyes from
one side to the other, looks, rejoices and is surprised. — [9] + we rejoice with it. — [10] it
is not counted. — [11] until they discover it; and. — [12] om. — [a] or : concern. — [13] because
of the joy there is in his heart. — [14] the. — [15] is. — [16] + and. — [17] his. — [18] om. —
[19] om. — [20] the minds. — [21] and joy. — [22] in us.

88. [1] says. — [2] om. — [3] the. — [4] you shall be invited.

88. † Lk 14:8-11.

a lower place; when he who has called you shall come (and) say,
'Friend, go higher up and sit', then there shall be glory for you before
all the guests; for everyone who exalts [5] himself shall be humbled [6],
and he who humbles [7] himself shall be exalted [8]'. ⌜And he spoke
this word, because he looked (and) saw [9] that they were seeking the [5]
first place. And in fact this ⌜same thing [10] is accomplished for the
Church; for our Lord is the lord of the guests and we are his guests who
were invited to the [11] banquet; and thus this same thing itself is
accomplished. But as the man ⌜when he [12] invites the guests, at
first he invites them with a word, and then afterwards they come (and) [10]
arrive at the [13] banquet, in like manner also our Savior at first invited
us with his Word and then afterwards we go to the banquet.

89. And [1] our Lord beheld (and) saw that they were seeking the
first place at the banquet : this [2] is accomplished among [a] us; for
today we hasten to be the chief leader, and we do not hasten to do [15]
the works worthy of the leadership. And today those who humble
themselves in the world are despised in our eyes; as also [3] our Lord
said, ⌜he says [4], 'He who ⌜shall exalt [5] himself, shall be humbled, †
and he who ⌜shall humble [6] himself, shall be exalted'. Therefore
⌜in fact [7] they sit down at the highest place, because they humbled [20]
themselves ⌜and kept the commands of their Lord [8]. Those whom
our Savior beheld (and) saw, that they were pressing and seeking
the first place at the banquet, they are those who hasten to advance
themselves to stand at the head of the people. And they themselves
chose this for themselves, and [9] their intentions [b] were ⌜not at all [10] [25]
just, but the choice was for themselves. But this is the choice of
God : when you shall keep and observe his commandments, and your
works shall be clear among men; when you shall not want that anyone
shall know your works which you do, except God; when [11] your
works themselves do not permit [12] you to be concealed, as the good [30]
works of our Lord do [13] not permit him to be concealed; and (the

---

[5] humbles. — [6] exalted. — [7] exalts. — [8] humbled. — [9] om. — [10] om. — [11] his. — [12] who.
— [13] his.

89.   [1] om. — [2] it. — [a] lit. upon. — [3] om. — [4] om. — [5] read : 'exalts' B. — [6] read :
'humbles' B. — [7] om. — [8] Moreover. — [9] even if. — [b] lit. thoughts. — [10] om. — [11] +
also. — [12] give. — [13] read : 'did' B.

89.   † Lk 14:11.

same applies) to the Prophets and to the Apostles.   Now such a person
is fit for leadership; for before he [14] shall have become ⌐a leader [15]
his works were [16] clear among men, and God (was) [17] glorified in him.

90.   When one becomes [1] such a chief [2] leader by his strength
5 and good works, so that he awakens many and many men are cured
by him, so that they repent [a] and live, because the leader stands
at the head of the people; ⌐and he [3] is like the physician, ⌐for the
physician cures the wounds [4] with his medicines, and [5] with the
medicine [6] the living Word of God, he heals broken hearts and troubled
10 souls.   And as the physician who [7] sees the wounds and with his
knowledge knows what medicine is necessary for it, in like manner
also the learned physician of the Church, when he sees someone whose
heart is broken ⌐and whose spirit is grieved, he knows what medicine
is necessary for him [8] in [9] the Holy Scriptures ⌐in order to heal [10]
15 him with comfort to the sufferings of his soul.   As [11] Moses, who [12]
became a leader, and he led righteously; and (who became) a shepherd,
and pastured well; and (who became) a physician, and healed the
people of Jacob with health.   Now such ⌐a leader [13] is becoming ⌐to
the leadership [14].

† 91.   Since our Savior said, ⌐he says [1], 'Pray and implore that
your flight shall not be in the winter nor on the Sabbath', he spoke
concerning the bitterness of the manifestations of the enemy, which
is coming upon the earth.   And heaven and earth and all creation
keep the Sabbath, for the tribulation is coming, and [2] the terrible
25 sound of the voices [3], and the horror and the terror upon the earth,
and the hands [4] of all men are disabled from the ⌐agitation of the
⊙ terror [5] of the voice.   Therefore he says, 'Pray, that your flight shall
not be in the winter, nor on the Sabbath', for the winter and the
Sabbath day came (and) reached upon him.   And God caused Jeru-
30 salem to keep the Sabbath, and he abolished [a] its sabbaths ⌐and its
laws [6], and the wicked justice [7] of its inhabitants at the final end

---

[14] they. — [15] leaders. — [16] are. — [17] is.

90.   [1] shall become. — [2] om. — [a] lit. turn to God. — [3] who. — [4] who heals the wounded. — [5] in like manner also. — [6] medicines. — [7] om. — [8] om. — [9] with. — [10] he heals. —
[11] + also. — [12] om. — [13] leadership. — [14] om.

91.   [1] om. — [2] om. — [3] voice. — [4] hearts. — [5] terrible sound. — [a] lit. stopped. —
[6] om. — [7] injustice.

91.   † Mt 24:20. — ⊙ Mt 24:20.

⌐of the days [8] of his crucifixion; and there was tribulation, and the
terrible sound of the voice, and the dread and fear of it upon the earth,
and the hands of [9] the disciples were disabled from ⌐the terror of the
fear [10], and the sun was darkened. Therefore he says, 'Pray that ◔
you may be worthy to escape from all those [11] things which are to be'. 5
As also [12] in his day when the Jews raised him on the cross, there was
the terrible sound of the voice, the fear and dread and [13] persecution
and sorrow of the disciples for their Lord. In like manner also, if
that day happens to us, the tribulation shall be upon us, and the
terrible sound of the voice, and the dread and the fear, and agitation 10
and persecutions, grief and sorrow for our Lord. And as ⌐to them [14]
in fact, the dawn of the morning was near to them for the good news
of the joy of their Lord; in like manner also if that day happens to
us [b], the dawn of the morning will be near to us for the good news
and joy of our Lord; as also our Savior said, he says, 'For the sake ☦
of the elect those days will be shortened'.

    92.   And moreover the more so, he says, 'There will be the groan- †
ing [a] of men from the agitation [b] (and) [1] fear, and from the terrible
sound of the voice as the sea that is agitated'. Therefore our Savior
precautioned us, for he pitied [2] us. And [3] as any man who might 20
bury fire in his house upon the lower (floor) and he shall sleep on the
upper (floor) of the house, it shall send forth much smoke [4], and the
smoke shall go up (and) reach to him by the holes in the floors and
through the gaps in the ceiling and the house shall be filled with
smoke, and the man shall awake with his [5] much fear and shall say 25
in his mind, 'Woe [6] to me and [7] what have I suffered? Perhaps my
fire which had been buried was kindled again'. In like manner also,
he is aware of Satan on account of the fire, that has been buried in
hell underground, that [8] was kindled in order to burn; therefore [9]
he is furious and is enraged, in order to destroy (and) exterminate 30
men, he together with his hosts.

---

[8] om. — [9] + all. — [10] before the fear and the terror. — [11] the. — [12] om. — [13] om. —
[14] om. — [b] lit. if we happen in that day.
    92.   [a] or : heaving of sighs. — [b] or : perplexity. — [1] and. — [2] cared for. — [3] om. —
[4] fire into the house. — [5] om. — [6] + is. — [7] om. — [8] and. — [9] + moreover the more
so he says, 'the groaning of men'.

    91.   ◔ Lk 21:36ab. —   ☦ Mt 24:22b.
    92.   † Lk 21:25-26a

†   93. Therefore our Lord commanded us and says, 'If they shall say to you, behold Christ is here, or ⌐he is ¹ there, do not go out, lest you be led away'; as the disciples (were) ² nowhere (around) ⌐on account of ³ the Jews when they raised him on the cross, but when he rose
5 from the dead, then they appeared and they escaped from their killers, and they saw him. Therefore before the rise of the Man of Wickedness, we must teach and admonish men (about) his ways, and his ⁴ deceits which he has prepared to work upon the earth; for he makes himself an imitator of God with all the ⁵ signs and miracles; for he ⁶ sends
10 him for the temptation ª of the world. Thus ⁷ God ⁸ gives to him
⊙ authority, as also Daniel himself said, he says, 'Over all gods and idols of worship ⌐he shall pride himself, and rise ⁹ with arrogance with false ¹⁰ signs and miracles and with temptations'. Even our Savior
◐ said, ⌐he says ¹¹, 'If possible ᵇ, ⌐he would lead astray ¹² many of the
15 elect'.

  94. Therefore it is necessary for us to precaution and to preach to ignorant men, for they are ignorant of the knowledge of the Scriptures; lest suddenly he should arise somewhere, ⌐and shall deceive ¹ with the signs which he works; for ² he imitates Christ himself, lest
20 they should follow him. And ⌐they are ³ required at our hands, unless we precautioned them; but we precautioned ⁴ them in this manner, that absolutely by no means should they believe anything in that ⌐sound of the ⁵ terrible voice from the dreadful fear which is coming ª, and in the wonders which they hear, lest they should
25 believe them ⁶, but in ⌐these signs ⁷ which are ᵇ coming in the heavens should they believe. When they shall see the sun and the moon that they shall be darkened and the sign which is coming in the heavens, this itself is the cross of light which is spread in the heavens, in this only should they believe, and in nothing else : as our Lord said, he
† says 'In those days after that tribulation, the sun shall be darkened

---

93. ¹ om. — ² read : 'appeared' B. — ³ om. — ⁴ om. — ⁵ add : 'false' B. — ⁶ read : 'God' B. — ª i.e. testing. — ⁷ om. — ⁸ he. — ⁹ and he rises and prides himself. — ¹⁰ om. — ¹¹ om. — ᵇ lit. if he could make the means. — ¹² to destroy.

  94. ¹ om. — ² and. — ³ it is. — ⁴ shall precaution. — ⁵ om. — ª lit. is to be. — ⁶ om. — ⁷ that sign. — ᵇ lit. is.

93. † Lk 17:23. — ⊙ Dan 11:36ab. — ◐ Mt 24:24b.
94. † Mt 24:29,30.

and the moon shall not give its light, and the powers of heaven shall
be shaken, and then the sign of the Son of Man shall appear in heaven,
and all the tribes of the earth shall see it, and the Son of Man; for he
shall come with the bright clouds'.   And when we precaution them,
it shall be fulfilled upon us [8] that which Daniel spoke, ⌐he says [9]. 5
'They who justify many shall shine as the stars of heaven'.   Because ⊙
⌐they say to men [10] the thing [11] which amazes the minds of men,
and his head reaches to the heavens, do not believe them, because
he is a man like us.   Daniel and the Prophets made clear concerning
him, for in that time when he perceived the vision of the kings, he 10
also named them : horns and beasts; moreover he also called those
same, beast and horn.   Therefore he is a man like us.   Behold also
Isaiah the Prophet says moreover, in the time when he was speaking
concerning the King of the Babylonians, he says, 'You said in your ◓
heart, I shall ascend into heaven, and above the stars ⌐of God [12] I shall 15
put my throne, and I shall dwell in the high mountain in the sides
of the north; and I will ascend to the heights of the clouds, and in
the likeness of the Most High I will be'; as a man he was like us,
nevertheless thus he was proud ⌐and was risen [13] and ascended in his
heart, for God raised him in order to chastise the earth through him. 20

95.   And moreover let us look to Moses, and to those who stood
in front of [a] him and made before him miracles and signs and ⌐wonders,
terrible temptations and spectacles of fear [1] which God gave for the
obstinate.   For he shall be glorious, through that which he had
worked, and his name shall be proclaimed in all places; as also [2] he 25
said, ⌐he says [3], 'For this reason I showed [4] you in front of me, so †
that I might tell you [b] my power [5] and my glory below all the heavens'.
And though they are men as we, nevertheless in this manner the
Scriptures ⌐make manifest [6] concerning them : that they ascended,
were proud and were presumptuous, with their great ⌐reign, power [7] 30
and tyranny over all creatures, and (concerning) the minister [8] who

---

[8] them. — [9] om. — [10] men say. — [11] that. — [12] om. — [13] om.

95.   [a] or : opposed. — [1] wondrous deliverances and spectacles of terrible fear. — [2] +
in fact. — [3] om. — [4] read : 'set' B. — [b] or : in you. — [5] my power might be told by you. —
[6] told. — [7] reign of power. — [8] ministers.

94.   ⊙ Dan 12:3. — ◓ Isa 14:13,14.
95.   † Ex 9:16 (Paraphrase).

is indeed called into the earth; and some (are) with power and signs
and wondrous spectacles ⌐and with terrible signs ⁹. In like manner
also the Man ⌐of Sin ¹⁰ who is to come at the end of the world, he is
a man like us, nevertheless powers and signs and temptations and
⁵ wondrous spectacles are to come through him ᶜ; as also the Lord
himself said, and not as many ¹¹ men say in ¹² their understanding;
they say ¹³ his head reaches to the clouds and he makes very great
signs. And if they ¹⁴ look to the signs of very great power, ⌐they
say ¹⁵, they will see in those things, which were contrary to Moses,
¹⁰ that in fact they made signs and wonders and terrible spectacles
before him.

96. Moreover because of ᵃ this our opposition they worked all
this; and that one who is coming, comes because of this opposition;
and very great signs are coming by him for the temptation of the
¹⁵ world, and because of the abundant iniquity which is in the earth,
he is sent with temptations, so that the world may be tried by him,
as also Daniel the true Prophet says. And perhaps someone might
say that what Daniel said was ¹ fulfilled by the Maccabeans and his
mind is taken away with this. However ² it should be known that
²⁰ in this manner only ³, whatever God created, he created two by two,
one over against the other; he created darkness over against light,
and death against life, and evil against good. Now everything which
has been created by him is ⁴ like this : they stand one over against
the other according to his glorious decree. In like manner also, the
²⁵ people of the Israelites ⁵ were our ⁶ examples ⁷; our behavior and our
religion were made through them, and there was variation between
people, and between altars, and between the Church and Jerusalem,
† and between laws; ⌐as also the Apostle says ⁸. 'As there was change
in his priesthood, thus also it was necessary for the law to be changed';
³⁰ although there is one Law, nevertheless the fulfillment of the law
is Christ. Therefore as in the sons of Israel our ⁹ laws and our ¹⁰

---

⁹ om. — ¹⁰ om. — ᶜ lit. by his hand. — ¹¹ om. — ¹² from. — ¹³ + that. — ¹⁴ + shall.
— ¹⁵ om.

96. ᵃ lit. by. — ¹ is. — ² om. — ³ he knows. — ⁴ om. — ⁵ Israel. — ⁶ the. — ⁷ + and.
— ⁸ in agreement with which the Apostle also writes. — ⁹ om. — ¹⁰ om.

96. † Heb 7:12.

behavior and the ways [11] of our worship were made ⌜through them [12]
previously, and we came (and) reached, and it was made (and) was
accomplished with us everything which the Holy Spirit showed on
our behalf through them as with signs.

97.   In like manner also the four kings of the house of Alexander, 5
⌜when they [1] arose and subdued all the land, and ruled over it, they
are the example of the four kings who are to come at the end of time;
they make clear that they invade and subdue, and devour all the land,
and rule over it.   And as Antiochus arose after them with a brazen-
face and with tyrannical power, and he arose (and) [2] ascended ⌜with 10
arrogance [3], ⌜agitation and [4] tyranny over everything which is [5]
indeed called gods and religion in the land of the Jerusalemites [6],
in like manner also (shall be) that one who is to arise at the end of the
four kings who are to arise [7], ⌜at the final end of the world; for [8] he
is indeed proud and rises over everything which is indeed [9] called 15
gods and [10] religion ⌜in the land [11].

98.   But [1] when the four kings shall arise according to the likeness
of the previous ones, then are [2] fulfilled, the sign [a] of [3] the image which
concerning them was made by them; for ⌜they showed [4] concerning
them before the time, as also we (were shown) by the Israelites.   And 20
in this manner ⌜we expect [5] that the desolations (will) be made in the
days of the four kings; as also Mark says in the Gospels, he says,
'When you shall see the abomination of desolation which shall stand †
in the place where it ⌜is not [6] proper, he who reads shall understand'.
And what is the interpretation of the abomination which it speaks 25
(of), except the shaking and trembling, and extirpation [7] and dissolu-
tion; for the sons of men ⌜are extirpated and are undone and are
shaken and wander [8] from place to place, after they have dwelt in
the desolation in which they indeed are made; and the hands of men
shall despair (of) what shall happen over all [9] the land; as also Mark 30
has written in the four-part Gospels; and [10] many wise (men) bring

[11] way. — [12] om.

97.   [1] who. — [2] and. — [3] and became arrogant. — [4] with. — [5] was. — [6] Jerusalem. —
[7] be. — [8] om. — [9] om. — [10] or. — [11] as also the Scriptures say.

98.   [1] Now. — [2] read : 'is' B. — [a] lit. indication. — [3] (and). — [4] it was shown. —
[5] it appears. — [6] shall not be. — [7] desolation. — [8] are shaken and wander and are undone. — [9] om. — [10] om.

98.   † Mk 13:14ab.

these [11] words over Jerusalem and the Gentiles, for ⌐they say the
renowned abomination [12], (was) at the time when they besieged it,
and it was desolated [13]. But since our Lord pitied [14] us, he made
clear ⌐to us [15] about Jerusalem, and he showed us also what is coming [b]
5 at the end; ⌐and when [16] he explained about Jerusalem, ⌐he spoke
⊙ in this manner to them, 'When you shall see (that) Jerusalem (is)
indeed surrounded with armies, then know that her desolation has
arrived'. And they [17] indeed surrounded Jerusalem [18], with armies
and it was desolated. And moreover Matthew speaks about this,
☽ 'When you shall see the abomination of the desolation [c] which shall
stand in the Holy place in Jerusalem; it was proclaimed by Daniel
the Prophet; he who reads shall understand'. Therefore we know
that Jerusalem was desolated, and all the things that the Prophets
spoke concerning it [19] were fulfilled.

15   99.   Now it is built by the Man of Sin, otherwise how is the deception
of the one who comes and deceives proved? Behold the Apostle
says, he said in his precaution concerning the last times, ⌐he says [1],
† 'Let no one deceive you, and by no means', if ⌐they say [2] (that) behold
the day of the Lord (has) [3] arrived, for (he shall not come) 'unless the
20 rebellion shall come first and the Man of Sin shall be revealed, the
son of perdition, the adversary; he [4] becomes arrogant over everything
what is called god or religion. For he comes (and) enters into the
temple of God ⌐to sit [5] and to make himself appear that he shall be
God'. And in what temple does he sit? Behold (is) it not in Jeru-
25 salem because of his deception [6]? 'Behold I am [7] Christ, that one
who the Prophets spoke concerning me [8]'. And ⌐what more shall
he say, for he shall sit [9] in their temple, for [10] he makes himself a
god to them [11]. This we know, that this one ⌐is in this manner because

---

[11] the. — [12] he says, the abomination is called. — [13] pillaged; and moreover this which
Matthew (MR : 'Luke') says over Jerusalem, 'when you shall see Jerusalem (that it is)
indeed surrounded, then know her desolation (Lk 21:20 — Paraphrase). — [14] cared
for. — [15] om. — [b] lit. to be. — [16] for after. — [17] it came to pass that it was. — [18] om. —
[c] or : destruction (lit. corruption). — [19] them.

     99.   [1] om. — [2] om. — [3] has. — [4] read : 'who' B. — [5] om. — [6] + and he says. — [7] +
the. — [8] him. — [9] this he says when he sits. — [10] and. — [11] the Jews. And.

98.   ⊙ Lk 21:20. — ☽ Mt 24:15 (Paraphrase).
99.   † II Thess 2:3,4.

he makes [12] himself a god, and ⌐sits according to the likeness [13].   Moreover in fact the Apostle made clear his deception now and what is
coming [a], in that he says, 'The mystery of the iniquity even already ☉
increases, even until the time that the prince shall be taken from the
midst, and then the Evil One, the son of perdition shall be revealed'. 5
Therefore by the indication of the words we know; for in regard to ☾
the Weeks, Daniel says, they repair and [14] build for Jerusalem the
public places and the streets at the end time; and sixty and two weeks
after Christ shall have died [15], the Holy City with destruction shall
be taken away, along with the king who is coming [b], and its end (shall 10
be) with the flood, even with the war of final destruction.

100.   And moreover concerning this same thing, that is, what
happens from this, which was done (and) accomplished, and what
happens from this one who still remains to come [a], ⌐and what still
remains to happen from that one [1], ⌐that is what Daniel spoke (of) [2], 15
that at his second coming our Lord will flood him [3].   Moreover who
is it, except that deceiver who is [4] seated ⌐with assurance [5] in it [b],
for he makes him into a flood of fire of [6] wrath; for in him judgment
is coming [c].   The more so Matthew said, 'When you shall see the †
abomination of desolation, which shall stand in the Holy place', 20
because of the desolation, which ⌐spoils and desolates and [7] arises
by the Wicked One; the Spirit made clear and showed through [8]
Matthew, through the memory of his mind, from [9] the mouth of his
Lord, he says, 'When you shall see that sign, then they who shall⌐ ☉
be in Judea, let them flee to the mountains'.   And who shall be 25
Judea, except the universal Church which was called Judea, ⌐and
(who) believed in it?   Because in fact it is Judea, for it is from the
people of Judah [10], and Judea named itself, and they who (were)
from it, were named Judea; and [11] he precautioned them.

---

[12] in this manner is to make. — [13] to sit in the temple of God. — [a] or : to be. — [14] read :
'(and)' B. — [15] been killed. — [b] or : to come.

100.   [a] lit. to be. — [1] om. — [2] om. — [3] + according to what Daniel spoke. — [4] shall
be. — [5] read : 'falsely' B. — [b] i.e. the temple. — [6] with. — [c] lit. to be. — [7] om. —
[8] to. — [9] and. — [10] om. — [11] om.

---

99.   ☉ II Thess 2:7,8a. — ☾ Allusion to Dan 9:25,26.
100.   † Mt 24:15a (Paraphrase). — ☉ Mt 24:15a,16.

101.   When you shall see, he says, the abomination of the desolation and the destruction of Jerusalem, for it is to arise in the flood ᵃ
of fire and in the temptation of the world, and in the decree ᵇ which
is coming by the iniquity [1]; (when) he says, 'Then you who shall be
⁵ in Judea', — ⌐he spoke (that) concerning his Church [2] — 'flee', ⌐he
says [3], 'into the mountains' [4].   ⌐And if anyone shall say [5] what ever
the Gospels said [6] concerning the end times, nevertheless [7] the Word
upon Jerusalem has been fulfilled, in the time when the armies surrounded it and ⌐they were destroyed [8]; ⌐in that way [9] which one
¹⁰ understands, ⌐in that way [10] he shall understand, for although all
the Prophets prophesied concerning our Lord, nevertheless the signs
were not like to each other, which they showed concerning him.   Some
made clear ⌐and showed concerning him [11], that he has been born
from a virgin; some showed about his [12] crucifixion; ⌐and some,
¹⁵ since he is coming with the clouds, showed concerning that [13]; and
all other persons, in this manner made clear and showed about something.   And he came, and [14] everything whatever they said concerning
him was done [15], was accomplished and was [16] verified by him.   In
like manner also, the words of our Lord which he spoke, ⌐the signs [17]
²⁰ have ⌐explained and separated [18], ⌐and they are not likened [19] to
one another [20], concerning the end times which [21] he showed to us;
for the Holy Spirit ⌐made clear and [22] showed at that time ⌐what
was to happen then in various places at the final end [23]; for from
men has [24] been hidden the approach of the time of their sorrow;
²⁵ as also it has been spoken.   And with mercy it is revealed to them who
are worthy to preach it at that time, ⌐each in his place [25]; and [26]
his [27] glory [28] shall be increased, as also the mouth of the Lord [29]
bore witness [30].

102.   Now the Spirit ⌐showed and made clear [1] through Mark
³⁰ according to the memory of the words of his Lord, that the desolations

---

101.   ᵃ See Dan 9:26. — ᵇ lit. election. — [1] read : 'Evil One' B. — [2] del : om B. —
[3] del : om B. — [4] add : 'he spoke (that) concerning his Church' B. — [5] he says. — [6] read :
'say' B. — [7] om. — [8] read : 'it was pillaged' B. — [9] But. — [10] according to this way. —
[11] om. — [12] the. — [13] om. — [14] om. — [15] + and. — [16] were. — [17] om. — [18] separated
and explained. — [19] om. — [20] + that which. — [21] om. — [22] om. — [23] what then at the
final end is to happen in various places. — [24] have. — [25] in each place. — [26] om. —
[27] the. — [28] + of the Lord. — [29] same. — [30] + when he said, 'This Gospel of the Kingdom
will be preached in all the world and then will come the end' (Mt 24:14).
   102.   [1] made clear and showed.

which are not proper are [2] to be made; and through Matthew he
made clear the desolation ⌈and destruction [3] of Jerusalem, for it [4]
is to arise in ⌈the deception [5] of the flood [a] of fire. ⌈Concerning this
time which is to arise then [b], and concerning Jerusalem, he explained
and made clear to us, also concerning those [6] ⌈who believed in him [7]. 5
'Then, when you shall see (that) Jerusalem (is) indeed [8] surrounded †
with [9] armies, know that her desolation has arrived'. ⌈And the
armies indeed surrounded it and it was desolated, as also he said [10].
And that desolation and wrath and tribulation which came (and)
arrived on it ⌈in its final days, is an example of the works of tribulation 10
which are to be for us next, (and it) was worked and was shown through
it [11]. Because he said to his believers, ⌈'Then when you shall see', ⊙
he says [12], 'the sign ⌈of the terror [13] of the desolation of Jerusalem',
⌈concerning which he has spoken, 'then', he says [14], 'you who shall
be in Judea [15]', who believed in me, that I myself am Judea, 'flee to 15
the mountains', before it shall have enclosed and encompassed you
with sufferings. And moreover this same thing returns and is accomplished upon us; for the Word which has been written turns to
both sides, as Israel indeed was turned to us; for we also should be
⌈ready and [16] watchful, so that when we [17] see the desolations which 20
are desolated from the wrath [18] that is [19] raised up and is [20] made
in order for many armies to gather, which ⌈are [c] brought together
and [21] go there - when you shall see this sign of terror [22], that great
tribulation that approaches and comes upon us, let us flee to the
mountains before we shall have fallen into (its) hands. ⌈For every- 25
thing whatever happened (and) [23] was worked previously, is our
example ⌈and work which was worked and was shown through them [24],
whether ⌈it shall be [25] good or evil, ⌈for by us all certainly shall be
fulfilled; as also the Spirit and the examination of the Scripture shows
and makes clear, as also it has been written [26].   30

---

[2] were. — [3] om. — [4] the deception. — [5] om. — [a] See Dan 9:26. — [b] or : presently. —
[6] om. — [7] For concerning the believers, he says, to those who were in that time. —
[8] om. — [9] + many. — [10] om. — [11] was an example of Great Tribulation which in the
final days is to be worked. — [12] om. — [13] om. — [14] om. — [15] + that is, those. —
[16] om. — [17] you shall. — [18] destruction. — [19] they. — [20] they. — [c] lit. is. — [21] having
gathered together. — [22] + know. — [23] Now as we said, what. — [24] om. — [25] om. —
[26] om.

102.   † Lk 21:20. — ⊙ Mt 24:15a,16.

103.　And as I believe, it seems to me that the desolations of Meso-
potamia are made in order to draw near to the end of the world,
as also it has been written in the Gospels in Mark; and after the desolations have been made, the report goes out to the world as with
† a sign after a short time. 'Behold here', they say ,'The Jews are
gathered', and know that they are gathered to false beliefs ¹, and
heretical authority. Woe shall be to that age, in which the four
kings shall arise according to the likeness of the previous ones; for
there remains hidden ᵃ in it, the weeping and lamentation and perse-
10 cutions and ⸢very great tribulations of ² bitterness; as for ³ heaven
and earth, they observe the Sabbath in that age. In that time in
which the ⁴ mind ⸢shall be ⁵ to itself, let us not do the works of the
world, but (let us) only pray and implore and supplicate, so that
one shall be able to escape and to flee, and overcome. For at the
15 final end of the four kings, all the kingdoms of the earth are troubled
and disturbed by the war ⁶ and the troops of the kings who shall ⁷
arise over all the earth according to the power of this air; ⸢as also it is
⊙ written ⁸. As moreover our Lord also said ⁹. 'Behold here, you
hear the sound ¹⁰ of war and the rumor ᵇ,¹¹ of war; in that time watch
20 that ¹² you be not troubled'.

　104.　And then the Tempter shall arise after the wars and the
troops, and there shall be for him a little time, and then he shall be
proud, as ¹ the Scriptures say; for he shall arise suddenly and destroy
many. For first ² is the arrival of the Tempter with the signs and
25 miracles and powers ³, with temptations and with wondrous and
terrible spectacles, for he comes ⸢having taken ⁴ the world captive
⸢in death ⁵; 'Behold here ⁶, I am ⁷ Christ', (he says) and all the Jews
believe in him, because their hearts are set on their ⁸ desolated lands ⁹.
† 'Behold here', they say, 'Christ comes, and we are all gathered'.
30 And according to their desire he comes, and there he gathers them,
⊙ as also the Apostle said, he says, 'Therefore God sends ¹⁰ to them

---

103.　¹ belief. — ᵃ lit. buried. — ² tribulations and very great bitterness. — ³ also. —
⁴ his. — ⁵ is. — ⁶ read : 'wars' B. — ⁷ om. — ⁸ om. — ⁹ add : 'he says' B. — ¹⁰ sounds. —
ᵇ lit. sound. — ¹¹ om. — ¹² and.
　104.　¹ + also. — ² om. — ³ power. — ⁴ read : 'to take' B. — ⁵ del : om B. — ⁶ add :
'he says' B. — ⁷ + the. — ⁸ om. — ⁹ land. — ¹⁰ read : 'shall send' B.

103.　† Allusion to Jewish writings? — ⊙ Mt 24:6ab.
104.　† Allusion to Jewish writings? — ⊙ II Thess 2:11,12a.

false power, so that they shall believe in the falsehood [11] and shall
be condemned ⌐by it [12]⌐. ⌐They believe in him [13], and then there
shall be great tribulation, grief and sorrow, fear and dread, and
agitation and very great fright, and [14] the sons of men shall be dis-
heartened so that they shall groan from the great [15] terrible fright [16]; 5
many of them become exhausted from the sound of the voice and
from the agitation from the fright, ⌐and from the coming [17] tribulation,
under all the heavens. And the fathers turn not to (their) sons,
nor the sons to (their) mothers, for ⌐all the souls [18] stand shuddered
⌐from their agitation [19], and the eyes of men have looked from one 10
side to the other from the sound of the quaking, and from the amazement of [20] the astonishing fear.

105. Woe shall be to them who shall be with child, and who shall
have sucking babes in those days; for those who shall be with child,
their children shall be cooked and spoiled in them; and they who 15
shall have sucking babes shall see the sufferings of their children [1].
⌐And the heavens and [2] the earth ⌐are desolated [3] with ruin in the
eyes of men, as the sea when its waves are agitated, from the fright
⌐which is to come to him; for in this manner all the creatures are
agitated by it [4], and heaven and earth mourn from it, because of the 20
Son [5] of God; for he passes them through heat, ⌐he examines and
cleans the believers and the elect ones. As gold, that enters into the
furnace of fire and is examined and tested and its distinction has
appeared; and when it goes out from the furnace of fire and is wetted
with water, then its distinction has doubly appeared; in like manner [6] 25
they pass through heat and are examined and are distinguished and
the sons of the Kingdom have appeared ⌐with powers, signs and
temptations [a,7] and with terrible spectacles ⌐and wonders [8] which
he does. He is the furnace of examination for us; and then ⌐after
this [9] he shall turn and shall wet us in the baptism of blood ⌐of the 30
sword [10] of [11] his sufferings, as [12] gold, ⌐when it [13] goes out of the
furnace ⌐of fire [14], and ⌐then it is wetted [15] afterwards with water,
and [16] it becomes beautiful and is brightened.

[11] lie. — [12] by believing in it. — [13] om. — [14] om. — [15] + and. — [16] add : 'and' B. —
[17] there shall be. — [18] they. — [19] om. — [20] and.

105.   [1] + and they die. — [2] for all. — [3] shall appear desolate and. — [4] om. — [5] read :
'sons' B. — [6] as gold which passes and is wetted with water and its beauty appears,
the believers. — [a] i.e. testings. — [7] with temptations of powers and signs. — [8] om. —
[9] om. — [10] om. — [11] with. — [12] + also. — [13] which. — [14] om. — [15] om. — [16] om.

106.   Therefore before the action ¹ of the Tempter it is necessary
for us to teach and to show innocent men, ⌐whose ears ² are ³ ignorant
of Scriptures; ⌐for there are many ⁴ who do not know that at first
the false Christ is to come, and then the ⌐Son of God comes after him ⁵.
5 For ⁶ unless we henceforth precaution ⁷, he shall suddenly arise ⁸
and their minds shall stumble after him, ⌐and they shall say, 'behold
here, this one would be Christ ⁹'.   In order for them to see the agitation and the fright, and ⌐for them ¹⁰ to hear concerning the powers
⌐and wonders which he does ¹¹, they shall be as they who will follow
10 the straight road; and they shall have ª a place, for they shall be
fellow-travellers, and they shall ⌐stand (and) ¹² look to the right
(and) ¹³ to the left, for ¹⁴ they shall not know what they should do
or by which road they should go, for they will not have ᵇ a leader
who shows them ¹⁵ the road ⌐on which they remain to the end ¹⁶,
15 in order ⌐for them ¹⁷ to know ᶜ,¹⁸ the sound of the terrible voice ¹⁹
⌐and the agitations ²⁰ and the fright, even the wonders ⌐which they
shall hear ²¹, for thus ²² unexpectedly he shall arise.   And every
man is turned to himself, in order to flee, to hide and to save himself ²³
from the ravage which is to come.
20   107.   And there shall be afterwards men whom we did not instruct
and show the signs ⌐and distinction of the end of the narrow road,
on which they came previously, so that their eyes are lowered ª.
When they look, they shall say, 'Perhaps this one is Christ or that
one shall not be', for want of a leader who will show them the signs
25 and the opening to the right road; because they labored and came
to him with fasts and prayers and righteousness of service and by the
crucifixion of their Lord — because for them he ascended on the
cross — and through the preaching of the Apostles.   If they go astray,
they are required of our hands; for we ate the first-fruits, which they
30 honored us in faithfulness, and we did not watch them.   But they

---

106.   ¹ read : 'rise' B. — ² who. — ³ shall be. — ⁴ and. — ⁵ the real one; and because
of the signs they believe in him, but we ate their first-fruits, and their fruits of sacrifice. —
⁶ om. — ⁷ add : 'them' B. — ⁸ be revealed. — ⁹ om. — ¹⁰ om. — ¹¹ about the sound of
the terrible voice and about the agitation and the fright which he makes, and they shall
say, 'Behold this one shall be the Christ, and. — ª lit. it shall happen for them. — ¹² om.
— ¹³ and. — ¹⁴ and. — ᵇ lit. be to them. — ¹⁵ om. — ¹⁶ in like manner also these that we
do not precaution, go astray. — ¹⁷ om. — ᶜ lit. see. — ¹⁸ read : 'see the works of deception
and to hear' B. — ¹⁹ voices. — ²⁰ om. — ²¹ om. — ²² om. — ²³ om.
   107.   ª lit. hung.

are the sheep of Christ, which he gave and he entrusted them to us
in order to pasture and keep them; and we pastured ourselves, and
did not keep them; as also it is written. And we like that flee and
hide ourselves in order to escape the ravage of the tribulation, fear,
(and) dread, and the groanings of men. And they who themselves 5
have not of the joy of this diligent disposition, know not the power
to confide in that will; although they hide in the invisible places,
nevertheless they themselves are lost because of the groaning of the
spirits which are lost, who were themselves of them before (those)
times [1].   10

108. ⌐Therefore it is necessary for us to persuade and to strengthen⌐
wherefore Christ was crucified, and he commended it to us, therefore
he said, he says [1], 'He who gathers not with me, indeed scatters'- †
to teach and to show ⌐and to send to preach [2] to the children of the
universal [3] Church before the flood and the ravage of heresy [a] which 15
is to come over the world ⌐in the examination and in the temptation [4],
and [5] we shall be innocent ⌐and pure [6]; and [b] in that time the gates
of the cities are shut, and the villages and the mountains are examined, and the passage of the roads and the bridges over the rivers
are closed ⌐for us according to the [7] authority of the [8] command ⌐of 20
his Word [9], so that no one shall be able to flee and escape from it.
And all this (is) for the elect of God, until [10] he judges and examines
us by suffering [c]. ⌐And then [11] the strength ⌐and the firmness [12] of
each of us shall be examined and judged. Therefore our Lord said,
⌐to those who are from him [13], that in that time they should be watchful 25
in order to flee to the mountains before they will be enclosed under
the sufferings; for before the sufferings, according to the way of the

---

[1] so that their eyes are lowered and they shall say, 'This one perhaps shall be the
Christ or he shall not be'. But because we ate their first-fruits and their fruits of
sacrifice, it is proper to show the right road, lest they go astray; for though we who
know the Scriptures hide in secret places, still our spirits are poured out and we are
lost because of the spirits which were entrusted to us, in not precautioning them before
the time.

108. [1] And because Christ who was crucified for us said. — [2] read : 'it is necessary'
B. — [3] om. — [a] or : corruption. — [4] in order to examine and test. — [5] but. — [6] om. —
[b] lit. for. — [7] because of the great. — [8] his. — [9] om. — [10] because. — [c] lit. tortures us
(but ᛃᚢᚱᚦᚢᚱᛖᛖ can also mean βασανιζει). — [11] For. — [12] om. — [13] to his (own).

108.   † Mt 12:30b.

Scriptures he comes, so that ⌐the world will believe in him ¹⁴, that
he really ¹⁵ is Christ.　For to the Jews, ⌐as at this time ¹⁶, he says ¹⁷,
'I was revealed in ¹⁸ the Book of the Prophets; for ¹⁹ you waited and
hoped for me beforehand'; and to us likewise, ⌐he says ²⁰, 'Behold,
5 I came with greatness, and ²¹ whereas in the past I came with lowness,
⌐now behold I come with greatness ²², and both were accomplished
by me'; and this ²³ mystery (is) in our minds, ⌐because when he arises,
that one who reasons ²⁴ he also divides the mind of each of us ²⁵ with
these ²⁶ mysteries ²⁷, some in this manner and some in that manner,
10 as also in ⌐these days ²⁸; for behold the tribulations that ²⁹ the mysteries shall ³⁰ agitate, have not come yet.

　　109.　Therefore the Apostle precautioned us when he said, ⌐he
† says ¹, 'Be not afraid and be not perplexed ᵃ to anxiety from the
⊙ terrible agitation', therefore he said to us, ⌐he says ², 'Henceforth
15 we know no one by the flesh ³, although we knew ⌐we knew Christ ⁴,
but henceforth ⁵ no more ⌐do we know (him) by the flesh ⁶'; because
of the coming of that one who is to come according to the likeness
of Christ, he spoke, lest they shall believe in him.　Because our Lord
Jesus Christ is revealed through the Spirit, and he comes in the heavens
20 in the flesh, ⌐and he judges ⁷ the living and the dead, ⌐in like manner
(it is) also with this heresy ᵇ, for he is coming according to the likeness
of Christ ⁸.　⌐'Behold here ⁹ first ¹⁰ I judge the living, and then the
dead ¹¹'; therefore ⌐that tribulation ¹² is ⌐severe and ¹³ bitter.　And ¹⁴
then after the great tribulation and trouble ¹⁵, there shall be very
25 little peace (and) joy ⌐in the desolation ᶜ, in the sufferings and in the
ignominy of the bitterness ¹⁶.

---

¹⁴ it is believed. — ¹⁵ om. — ¹⁶ om. — ¹⁷ + Behold. — ¹⁸ according to. — ¹⁹ how. —
²⁰ om. — ²¹ om. — ²² om. — ²³ + as. — ²⁴ om. — ²⁵ + he agitates. — ²⁶ + heretical. —
²⁷ + and he turns. — ²⁸ this day. — ²⁹ and. — ³⁰ om.

　　109.　¹ om. — ᵃ or : agitated. — ² om. — ³ + for. — ⁴ read : 'Christ by the flesh' B. —
⁵ del : om B. — ⁶ in the same manner. — ⁷ to judge. — ᵇ or : corruption. — ⁸ but he who
is to come according to the likeness of Christ, with this heresy. — ⁹ om. — ¹⁰ add : 'he
says' B. — ¹¹ add : 'and' B. — ¹² the agitation. — ¹³ om. — ¹⁴ om. — ¹⁵ agitation. —
ᶜ lit. corruption. — ¹⁶ from the desolations, which in the bitter ignominy they make
sufferings.

　　109.　† Allusion to II Thess 2:2 ?　⊙ II Cor 5:16.

110.   And when [1] the beginning of the measure ⌜shall be [2] fulfilled, which is given to him for the examination and temptations, the Jews shall answer him and shall say, 'When does our Lord God your Father †
raise up the dead, and we see our fathers and our brothers? for we waited and hoped for you for ages; and our Prophets who prophesied [3]   5
⌜concerning your first (coming and) [4] your present coming. And you judge the dead, and we are avenged of our enemies, who desolated [5] our holy [6] sanctuary [a], who [7] trampled and profaned it, and they took (and) cast us from the midst of it, and we were scattered everywhere and to the cities, according to the goodness of our God, 10 whom our Fathers angered with their strife'.

111.   And while they ⌜shall speak [1] this, the mark of the sign of the cross of our Lord appears in the heavens.   And when they see (it), they stand astonished, amazed, bewildered [2], staggered (and) frightened; and they shall lower their eyes [3] and [4] they shall indeed be 15 fallen upon their faces upon the ground, in shame and in fear and in lamentation.   And then the persecuted and the tormented and [5] the worked and the labored who shall be (there) in that time, (shall) lift up their heads to the good news of their Lord, within the caves, in which they shall be hidden; in the caves and in the caverns and in 20 the holes of the ground [6], in all parts of the hiding places, for they see in the heavens the mark of the sign of his cross.   And the grief of their sorrow becomes submerged in joy [7], to fly into the air of the heavens, as the young doves when ⌜their wings shall first [8] appear [9], they will want to fly and they shall not be able [10]; at first they shall 25 flutter (their) wings, and then they shall rise [11].

112.   Now thus [1] we should be watchful ⌜and we should be [2] clothed with activity [a] all the time, with labors and vigilance and care and [3] reflection [4] by day and by night, with [5] diverse signs ⌜and miracles [6], whatever is written in the Scriptures recently [7], which is to be revealed 30

110.   [1] then. — [2] is. — [3] + beforehand. — [4] om. — [5] ravages. — [6] om. — [a] lit. holiness. — [7] and.

111.   [1] spoke. — [2] om. — [3] + to the earth. — [4] om. — [5] om. — [6] + and they come. — [7] add : 'and their souls having been elevated rejoice' B. — [8] they first shall have wings. — [9] and. — [10] + but. — [11] fly.

112.   [1] om. — [2] (and). — [a] or : vigilance. — [3] om. — [4] we should reflect. — [5] on the. — [6] om. — [7] add : 'and' B.

110.   † Allusion to Jewish writings?

to us. As also Noah, for [8] he labored and watched with vigilance [b] for the ⌐signs of the time [9], which was commanded to him. And as Abraham, for he was watchful and waited for his good news and he had hope. And as Job, for he was watchful in the temptations [c] of
5 his righteousness and kept patience in his vigilance, in his temptations, ⌐in the work and labor of his righteousness [10]. And as Moses, for he was watchful with his mercy, and with the prayers of his supplications for the people, to whom he was the leader. And as Aaron in his praises. And as Daniel and his companions with the vigilance of
10 their faith. Thus all the prophets were watchful in something according to the works which had been given to them. Therefore [11] in like manner also we who were founded upon them, ⌐for we also [12] should be watchful like them with ⌐labors, vigilance [13], and [14] reflection ⌐by day and by night [15] on the signs of the times, and on their forms,
15 and moreover on the form of the signs which ⌐are to come [d] and [16] unexpectedly astonish us. For we shall be cleansed ⌐by them from this day in our minds, lest that day shall arise for us unexpectedly [17], and we shall not be found ready [18] in that [19] day.

113. If [1] anyone shall say that, 'not in my years, and not in these [2]
20 days; for the day that I die, ⌐that in fact [3] is my day'; ⌐in fact [4] such a person who says that [5] sleeps and has [6] become blind, and is overcome with sin, and (has) not repented; ⌐and as that one who [7] ⌐shall neglect [8] the tradition which was transmitted to him, he is [9] also unexpectedly deprived of it, for he was [10] not watchful, and he does
25 not awaken in this ⌐time of [11] war; as also our [12] Lord said to Simon,
† he says, 'Awake and keep your brothers [13]'. For everyone who loves the world ⌐and delicate garments [14] and excellent foods, and possesses [15] beautiful vessels, such a person is the servant of sin ⌐and is its minister [16]; though he should be excessively poor, he also [17]
30 ⌐has envied [a,18] the world and ⌐shall not have envied [19] the spiritual

---

[8]om. — [b] or : activity. — [9] times and the sign. — [c] i.e. testings. — [10] om. — [11]om. — [12] om. — [13] vigilant labors. — [14] om. — [15] by night and by day. — [d] lit. to be. — [16] om. — [17] by diligence. — [18] honorable. — [19] + careless.

113.   [1] But if. — [2] om. — [3] even that. — [4] om. — [5] this. — [6] (has). — [7] he. — [8] neglects. — [9] read : 'shall be' B. — [10] read : 'is' B. — [11] om. — [12] the. — [13] + awake. — [14] om. — [15] om. — [16] om. — [17] om. — [a] lit. desired. — [18] envies. — [19] not.

113.   † Lk 22:32 ? (Agraphon ?)

road to heaven; as also it is written, ⌐he says ²⁰, 'The flesh desires ⊙
what injures the Spirit, and the Spirit desires what is not the will of
the flesh; and both are opposed to each other'.   And Paul the Blessed,
the Prophet and Apostle ⌐according to the decree of our Lord ²¹,
explained and said, 'For if you walk with the Spirit and act ⌐with ◗
the Spirit ²², not that ²³ you will do everything which you would like
(to do); not that we ⌐have not ²⁴ power for this ²⁵, but lest the Holy
Spirit which (has) ²⁶ dwelt in us be grieved, and he shall ²⁷ accuse
us to God'.   For the Son of God Jesus Christ and the Prophets and
the Apostles who came into the world, not that they resisted out- 10
wardly but inwardly, those who abandoned the truth and did not
trust.   But let us serve the Holy Spirit with purity, with solitude ᵇ
and ²⁸ with vigilance, and let us take ourselves to the mirror of the
Scriptures and let us see ourselves by it; and whatever stains, marks
and leprosy of wickedness there ⌐shall be on us ²⁹, let us clean and 15
wash from us, lest even we be found abject as they, ⌐for they ³⁰ took
not themselves to vigilance.

    114.   Now let us be watchful ⌐from this day after ¹ for the mani-
festation (and) ² coming of the sedition which is ⌐to be revealed ³
⌐upon the earth ⁴ with diverse forms ⁵; and let us inherit this vigilance 20
and proneness to diligence, for those who are to follow us.   ⌐For
when there is war, the trumpet is sounded for it; and moreover this
same trumpet (that) sounds for it, also calls the warriors.   And the
two sounds are from the trumpet, and their sounds are separated
(and) divided from each other; the first sound invites to greatness, 25
and the other to war; though ᵃ it is one; as also it is written in the
Law of Moses and in Jeremiah the Prophet ⁶.

    115.   Then it is necessary for us from this day after ⌐to arm, to
prepare ¹, and to get ready to oppose that one who is ⌐armed, prepared
and ² ready before ᵃ us, with diverse ⌐means and ³ deceits, with signs 30
and miracles of his powers in order to frighten us ⌐suddenly with
very great temptations ⁴.   For at first in the beginning of his mani-

---

²⁰ om. — ²¹ om. — ²² om. — ²³ om. — ²⁴ read : 'shall not have' B. — ²⁵ that. — ²⁶ has.
²⁷ om. — ᵇ or : monastic life. — ²⁸ om. — ²⁹ are. — ³⁰ who.
    114.   ¹ hereafter. — ² and. — ³ to come. — ⁴ om. — ⁵ signs. — ᵃ lit. when. — ⁶ om.
    115.   ¹ om. — ² om. — ᵃ or : against. — ³ om. — ⁴ om.

    113.   ⊙ Gal 5:17ab.   ◗ General reference to Paul; see Gal 5:16-17; Eph 4:30; etc.

festation he comes with signs [5], temptations, powers [6] and terrible
spectacles. Even [7] his powers and signs and spectacles are [8] the
example ⌜of the spectacle [9] which ⌜he shows for fear, and as [10] the
enchanters, who show only the spectacle and the example, ⌜and what
5 ever they show with the spectacle and the example, they show with
these [11], for they [12] obeyed them [13] and did their will, ⌜and they [14]
submit to them everything [15] whatever ⌜they want to show [16] in the
world : if it shall be with [17] fire, ⌜it ᵇ submits [18] to them; and [19] if
there shall be someone dead, ⌜to die or ᶜ to be live [20], is given into
10 their hands; whether it shall be with snakes, or whatever ⌜it shall be,
as [21] the Scriptures show; ⌜and in the eyes of men these are as a real
miracle [22]. Now [23] in this manner also ⌜that one who is the source
of that flood which is to be manifested, this same one operates the
powers [24] and shows a miraculous example [25] of spectacles (and)
15 signs [26]; whatever he wishes to show, ⌜they are [27] given into his
hands [28]; whatever miracles he shows, he shows with them; ⌜for this
(one) is, and for all who wish, he imitates for the sake of the fear
of the elect [29]. Therefore Paul [30] says his powers and signs are false.

116. And then Elijah shall follow him [1], to bring back ⌜the hearts
20 of all mortals to God; (and) [2] the Jews, lest they believe in him [3];
⌜and the world all returned, lest they be destroyed [4]; as also it is
† written, 'First Elijah ⌜shall come, so that he [5] shall prepare everything'.
And this is the preparation ⌜which Elijah prepares, for [6] ⌜he brings
back [7] the hearts of all [8] men to God; ⌜if they [9] listen to him. For he
25 is sent into the world with mercy, ⌜lest they be destroyed; for they
shall confirm [10] ⌜and shall stand [11] in the faith and shall endure in the
great tribulation, and they shall ⌜not believe in [12] him. And then
after the signs and the power [13] and temptations which he makes,

---

[5] + of. — [6] om. — [7] And. — [8]+ according to. — [9] om. — [10] they show. — [11] om. —
[12] + who. — [13] om. — [14] they also. — [15] om. — [16] is . — [17] om. — ᵇ lit. they. —
[18] read : 'it submits' B. — [19] om. — ᶜ lit. and. — [20] from death, life. — [21] om. — [22]
about the enchanters who were operating in the eyes of men. — [23] om. — [24] he operates
by these powers which are the source of these floods. — [25] examples. — [26] add : 'and'
B. — [27] read : 'it is' B. — [28] add : 'and' B. — [29] om. — [30] + in fact.

116. [1] them. — [2] om. — [3] + and the hearts of all men to God. — [4] om. — [5] having
come. — [6] (and). — [7] the turning back (of). — [8] om. — [9] they who. — [10] that the shaken
shall not fall but shall be confirmed. — [11] om. — [12] reject. — [13] read : 'powers' B. —

116. † Mk 9:12a.

he turns to destroy everything that he finds, with diverse sufferings
which shall be invisible to our eyes. Therefore our Lord said, ⌐he
says [14], 'For the sake of the elect those days shall be shortened'. And ⊙
the angels of heaven shall lament very [15] great sorrow for all [16] men.

117.   And then when [1] the tribulations shall [2] cease [3], the sun and   5
the moon shall be darkened, and the stars of [4] the heavens shall be
moved and shaken. And ⌐then his sign shall appear in the sky, the
cross of light, which is [5] spread in the heavens for a seven-day period.
And then [6] nations ⌐shall lament [7] over nation with distraction [8],
with amazement ⌐at the [9] fear and fright, ⌐and at the agitation and [10]   10
the perversion ⌐which shall be perverted [11], ⌐because they opposed [12]
us.

118.   The more so our Lord said [1], ⌐'In that day in which the Son   †
of Man is revealed [2], ⌐in that time [3] if anyone shall be on the roof
and his possessions shall be in his [4] house, let him not descend [5] to   15
take thence [6]; and he who shall be in the field, in like manner let him
not return back; remember the wife of Lot; he who wants [7] to save
his soul, shall lose it; and he who loses [8] ⌐his soul [9], he shall find it'.
And our Lord [10] said this [11] because we should always be watchful,
waiting and hoping, for those who are sent ⌐for us [12], in order to take   20
us away before him [13], every day and every night (for) that Sunday
on which he enters. Whether we shall be on the roof or somewhere [14]
outside, we shall be ready; ⌐and if we shall be [15] with great precaution,
let us also [16] raise our eyes ⌐to the East [17] to the high heavens, in
order to look for the sign of the cross [18] ⌐every day and every night [19];   25
for [20] our Lord is to be revealed. And let us persevere, and [21] have
ourselves ready ⌐with great precaution every day and every night [22],
for that Sunday in which he enters.

---

[14] om. — [15] om. — [16] om.

117.   [1] om. — [2] om. — [3] + and. — [4] in. — [5] the bright cross remains. — [6] om. —
[7] are upset. — [8] + and. — [9] with. — [10] because of. — [11] om. — [12] with which they were
opposing.

118   [1] says. — [2] om. — [3] when (there is) a cry. (?) — [4] read : 'the' B. — [5] turn. —
[6] it. — [7] read : 'shall want' B. — [8] read : 'shall lose' B. — [9] (it) for my sake. — [10] he. —
[11] + to us. — [12] om. — [13] the Lord. — [14] om. — [15] om. — [16] om. — [17] del : 'om' B. —
[18] + in the East. — [19] om. — [20] + there. — [21] (and). — [22] om.

116.   ⊙ Mt 24:22b.
118.   † Lk 17:30bc-33.

119. And let us not return to take something, because naked we are to rise ⌜in ᵃ soul ¹, in spirit ² and in body; as also ³ Elijah, ⌜for naked ⁴ he ascended ⌜(and) was taken away ⁵ into the heavens ⌜in soul, spirit and body ⁶, for he did not take any garments with 5 him; ⌜and that he took nothing with him is clear ⁷, for even ⁸ the mantle ᵇ which he once had, that also he left here ⁹. And perhaps at the time we might want to return to take one thing, then ¹⁰ we ⌜shall be ¹¹ found deprived to the depredation of (our) joys, and our labors and endurement of great ¹² tribulation which we endured shall 10 be lost; and thenceforth ¹³ we ¹⁴ shall be carried away instead of to the high heavens, ⌜we shall be carried away ¹⁵ to the underground pits; as also the wife of Lot, who despised and transgressed the commandment. ⌜And moreover ¹⁶ let us not be afraid of the agitation at the shaking of the earth, for it is shaken and is agitated and trembles, 15 ⌜and of ¹⁷ the sound of the thunder and ⌜the inevitable crash and ¹⁸ the lightning, which are to come upon us in that time ⌜on account of the trumpet ¹⁹, for ⌜it shall call and shake ²⁰ the underground pits of the abyss, so that they awake in it, everybody ⌜who sleeps ²¹ in the ground.

20 120. ⌜For in this manner our people are allegorized, and this means is fulfilled for our invitations to the wedding of the bride and the bridegroom. And as a virgin that shall be betrothed to the bridegroom, and that last day shall approach, for which she waited and hoped and longed for before her approach to the bridegroom, and that night 25 shall be in the heart of both of (them); and she labors and watches and works in the joy of her mind every night, and sleep is cut from her eyes, in the anxieties and exhilaration of (her) mind with the joy of her heart, and she waits and expects that the time immediately shall be dawned, so that she shall go to present herself before the 30 bridegroom, and having come to (him) she shall be enclosed in his bosom unadorned ᵃ, and the bridegroom shall rest and become joyful with her, with her beauty and the sweetness of her chastity and her understanding and the good condition of his bride, and she has do-

---

119. ᵃ lit. with. — ¹ naked. — ² + soul. — ³ om. — ⁴ when. — ⁵ om. — ⁶ om. — ⁷ om. — ⁸ om. — ᵇ or : cloak. — ⁹ there. — ¹⁰ om. — ¹¹ are. — ¹² om. — ¹³ om. — ¹⁴ it. — ¹⁵ we are plunged. — ¹⁶ om. — ¹⁷ from. — ¹⁸ om. — ¹⁹ om. — ²⁰ the call of the trumpet shakes. — ²¹ whoever slept.

120. ᵃ or : naked.

minion over all the treasures of her husband, of the small and of the
great.   Accordingly in like manner also, because we are betrothed
to the bridegroom, who is himself Christ the King, by his Father, with
his own blood from ancient times; and when the last day approaches,
in which there shall be one night for the Sunday to dawn, in our hearts 5
and in the heart of the bridegroom, in like manner we shall have
labored and watched and with anxiety and exhilaration of (our) minds,
with the joy in our minds, so that the sleep shall be cut from our
eyes; and we shall have lifted up our eyes to the heavens every night
with expectation, for we wait and hope and long, that behold he was 10
revealed.   Thus we shall speak to each other all the night, in which
our Lord is revealed [1].

121.   ⌜And there shall come to pass the starting, rising and mounting
one by one every night [1], of the sound of the thunder and the crash [2]
⌜and with [3] the shaking and with [4] the turbulence [a].   And [5] brother 15
shall say to [6] brother, when ⌜he shall have [7] been frightened [8], ⌜'At
this time [9] this name remained with me, and I do [10] not know how it
happened'.   And when he shall say this, the other also [11] shall say,
'At this time even my brother remained with me, and I do not know
how it happened'.   ⌜For many others also shall speak in this manner [12]. 20
Therefore ⌜that which he said to us, he says [13], 'He who shall be on †
the roof, ⌜or shall be outside somewhere [14], let him not return ⌜to
take away something from his house [15]', ⌜lest when [16] while he shall
want to take one thing, he ⌜shall be [17] deprived to the depredation
⌜of (his) joys [18], and ⌜shall [b] lose [19] himself.   And moreover this same 25

---

[1] And we come to the bridegroom whom we longed for; for as sleep is cut from the
eyes of the bride, and every night she longs for the morning that she shall present
herself to the bridegroom, in like manner also we are betrothed to the bridegroom
Christ by his Father beforehand : when the last day approaches for the Sunday to
dawn, we labor and watch and with anxiety (and) the joy of our minds we shall cut
sleep from our eyes and we shall lift our eyes to the heavens with longing and we will
continually say to each other that behold he is revealed, even in the night in which
our Lord shall be revealed.

121.   [1] om. — [2] brightness. — [3] of. — [4] om. — [a] or : agitation. — [5] om. — [6] + his. —
[7] having. — [8] + and he says. — [9] om. — [10] did. — [11] om. — [12] And this happens to
many. — [13] it was said to us. — [14] om. — [15] back. — [16] for. — [17] is. — [18] om. — [b] MR of
Codex A is used here (instead of 'he loses'). — [19] loses.

121.   † Paraphrase of Mt 24:17,18a or Mk 13:15,16a.

⊙ thing Luke shows, in the Gospels, ⌐for he says²⁰, he says, 'In this
night²¹ there shall be two in one bed; the one they shall take (and)
restore²², and the one they shall leave; ⌐there shall be two who²³
shall grind at one mill, the one they shall take ⌐(and) restore²⁴, and
5 the one they shall leave; and²⁵ there shall be two in the²⁶ field, the
one they shall take, and the one²⁷ ⌐they shall leave²⁸'. ⌐And it
● says²⁹, 'Where the body ᶜ is, there also the eagles will be gathered
together'. And as the eagles, that are gathered together and ⌐they
fly and³⁰ they soar into the high heavens over the meat³¹ which
10 they see, in like manner also we are compared to eagles, and our
Lord to the body; for the³² angels are brought to us ⌐on all the winds
and to all parts ᵈ, and³³ they soar and fly into the high heavens, to
carry us before our Lord, who is compared to the body and we to
the eagle³⁴, before the fury of the flaming fire, and³⁵ the sound of
15 the great trumpet and the flute ᵉ which the archangel urges ᶠ, ⌐with
praises to his Father and³⁶ with the hosts of his³⁷ angels, in that
night in which the bridegroom is revealed ⌐to her³⁸. At the dawning
of the Sunday, he sends all his bridal men and friends to take (and)
carry ⌐the bride³⁹ before the bridegroom in order to be placed in
20 his⁴⁰ presence, ⌐before the⁴¹ praises and ⌐the sound of the trumpets,
at which the bridegroom is to come, at the sound of praise to the glory
of the noble (one) with the hosts of the angels⁴². And then when
our eyes see our hope and inheritance, with love ⌐and bubbling spirit⁴³
and longing and labors and our battles ᵍ we sit with him on the bright
25 clouds, and he shall lift us on high with them, through great sacri-
fices⁴⁴ in order ⌐for us⁴⁵ to appear before the face of ⌐our Creator⁴⁶,
who is the Lord of glory, ⌐after the judgment⁴⁷; as he promised us
☩ and said, ⌐he says⁴⁸, 'Happy ⌐shall it be⁴⁹ for them who are pure
in ʰ heart, for they shall see God'.

²⁰ om. — ²¹ + if. — ²² raise. — ²³ and if two. — ²⁴ in order to restore. — ²⁵ + if.
²⁶ one. — ²⁷ other. — ²⁸ shall be left. — ²⁹ om. — ᶜ or : carcass. — ³⁰ having flown. —
³¹ food. — ³² all. — ᵈ or : regions. — ³³ to all parts and on all the winds. — ³⁴ eagles. —
³⁵ at. — ᵉ or : fife. — ᶠ or : presses. — ³⁶ om. — ³⁷ om. — ³⁸ read : 'And' B. — ³⁹ om. —
⁴⁰ the. — ⁴¹ of his. — ⁴² at the coming of the bridegroom, with the sound of the
trumpet, the hosts of the angels give praise to the glory of the noble (one). — ⁴³ om. —
ᵍ or : wars. — ⁴⁴ read : 'glory' B. — ⁴⁵ om. — ⁴⁶ him. — ⁴⁷ om. — ⁴⁸ om. — ⁴⁹ (is it). —
ʰ lit. with.

121. ⊙ Lk 17:34-36. — ● Lk 17: 37b. — ☩ Mt 5:8.

122. And ⌜they indeed confirmed ¹ to us that which the Scriptures say, that our people are after the fashion of the bride. John showed and made clear concerning the ⌜wedding ᵃ and its grandeur ᵇˑ², which was (discussed) previously; and Luke ⌜showed and ³ made clear about the last day, in which ⌜having ascended ⁴ they are taken away ₅ before the bridegroom. Accordingly happy ᶜ (is it) ⁵ for those who endure the Great Tribulation, ⌜who strive ⁶ more than the ancients ⁷ for the ⁸ Day of the Lord with the angels ⌜in heaven ⁹ in the splendor of glory. ⌜And let it not be that anyone shall ¹⁰ despise ¹¹ of the wise ⌜on account of that which ¹² is written, for the spirit ¹³ of the ₁₀ Prophets obeys; ⌜as also it is written ¹⁴. And ⌜if anyone despises ¹⁵, he should look at the sons of Israel, for ¹⁶ having become proud they had boasted and said, 'we are wise and ⌜we have ¹⁷ the Scriptures', ⌜and they were reading ¹⁸ as we. ⌜'Behold', they say ¹⁹, 'Christ comes'; and he came and they knew him not, ⌜because they were ₁₅ asleep; and ²⁰ ⌜the Prophets ²¹ were crying ⌜to them ²² concerning their Lord that he is coming. Now ²³ in this manner also, if we shall not look for the approaching of the time of his coming, ⌜we also shall (start to) awake and look about ²⁴ and awake, and (we will see that) we have been rejected (and) cast out ²⁵ according to their example. ₂₀ ⌜Even the Apostle said to us concerning them, 'Those things were †‌ an example for us ²⁶, ⌜lest we ²⁷ be desirous ⌜of iniquity ²⁸, as ⌜some of them desired ²⁹'. And moreover he says, 'The end of the world ⊙ has arrived upon us'.

123. Therefore happy shall it be for them who shall be watchful ₂₅ from this day after ⌜with righteousness for the revelation of their Lord; for they are grown strong ¹. ⌜Even as he ² says, 'Pray that †‌

---

122. ¹ it is indeed confirmed. — ᵃ or : marriage. — ᵇ lit. greatness. — ² the grandeur of the wedding. — ³ om. — ⁴ om. — ᶜ or : blessed. — ⁵ read : 'shall it be' B. — ⁶ for they long. — ⁷ ancient martyrs (or : witnesses). — ⁸ + final. — ⁹ om. — ¹⁰ But let not anyone. — ¹¹ add : 'these sayings' B. — ¹² because it. — ¹³ spirits. — ¹⁴ om. — ¹⁵ the despiser. — ¹⁶ who. — ¹⁷ om. — ¹⁸ they read. — ¹⁹ They who say, 'Behold. — ²⁰ om. — ²¹ by the Prophets who. — ²² om. — ²³ om. — ²⁴ having also awakened, we shall look about. — ²⁵ om. — ²⁶ For their example was for us, as Paul says. — ²⁷ let us not. — ²⁸ om. — ²⁹ they.

123. ¹ and they shall wait for the Lord. — ² who.

---

122. † I Cor 10:6. — ⊙ I Cor 10:11b.
123. † Lk 21:36ab.

you may be worthy to escape from all those things which are to be'. Because he knew the infirmity of the weakness of the faith of men, that they are not able to resist the Tempter; thus he spoke.   Therefore happy shall it be for them who shall have the intelligence ᵃ and shall
5 understand in those days, in which the four kings ⌐are to ³ arise at the end of the world, ⌐to build (and) establish, having affirmed in buildings and in plants of the world, the Apostles and their preaching ⁴, ⌐which there also they taught to the spiritual men, that they should be of one mind, and equal; whether they shall be wealthy or shall
10 be poor, everything of theirs shall be in common together, before there shall have come devastation, ravage and destruction for all the Churches ⁵.   ⌐And they shall persevere through fasts ⁶, prayers, ⌐sack cloth and ashes, night and day ⁷, with ⌐very great ⁸ supplications, ⌐so that they shall be worthy ⁹ to flee before the great ¹⁰
15 wrath ⌐and terrible spectacles which are to come, in order to flee before it ¹¹, or else ¹² to be strong ᵇ and to establish many.   And their praises shall indeed ᶜ be multiplied more than the first and the last, for they save men from before the kindled fire of the flood which is to come upon the heretical deception of men; having trusted in their
20 gold and silver, they confided in them more than in God; and upon all the sensualities ᵈ of them who (are) in the world, there shall be prepared for them the bride and sacrifice of fire from the refuge of them who trusted in it to escape through it. Senseless, foolish, feeble and wavering man who does not understand; know you not
25 that the food ᵉ which you eat day by day, that part and share is thine? You have the Scriptures and you read it for the reproach and admonition of yourself, lest he find you excusing yourself. And you look not to the foundation of the Apostles and the Prophets upon which you were built, and he resembled them.
30   124.   Now let us arise in behalf of ourselves, and let us immediately reach to our wills; and let us make war against pride, arrogance, doubt and envy, which have dwelt in us, for they are the enemies of our lives; and let us gain our lives immediately, which is in our God according to all the Scriptures.   To Christ eternal praises, Amen.

ᵃ or : mind. — ³ om. — ⁴ for they shall be able to build and establish the plant of the Apostles which is shaken. — ⁵ om. — ⁶ Now with. — ⁷ and. — ⁸ om. — ⁹ let us seek. — ¹⁰ om. — ¹¹ om. — ¹² om. — ᵇ Codex B ends abruptly at 'strong'. — ᶜ *բազմեալ* can also mean *շատացած* (see Arm. Dict., Venice, 1865). — ᵈ or desires. — ᵉ or : bread.

APPENDIX A

QUOTATIONS IN THE ORDER THEY OCCUR

APPENDIX B

QUOTATIONS IN THE ORDER OF THE
BOOKS OF THE BIBLE

D/1968/0602/26

Imprimerie Orientaliste, s.p.r.l., Louvain (Belgique)